From *Princess* TO PORN STAR

A REAL-LIFE CINDERELLA STORY

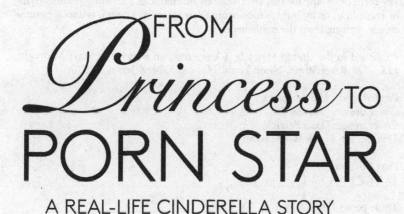

FROM *Princess* TO PORN STAR

A REAL-LIFE CINDERELLA STORY

TASHA REIGN

CLEiS
PRESS

Published in the United States by Cleis Press, an imprint of Start Midnight, LLC, 221 River Street, Ninth Floor, Hoboken, New Jersey 07030.

Printed in the United States
Cover design: Jennifer Do
Cover image: Dana Patrick
Text design: Frank Wiedemann

First Edition.
10 9 8 7 6 5 4 3 2 1

Trade paper ISBN: 978-1-62778-325-5
E-book ISBN: 978-1-62778-538-9

TABLE OF CONTENTS

*Dedicated to all the women
who have a curious mind and a big heart.*

*To all the sex workers who preceded me and all the
sex workers who will come after me. To all the women
who have used their bodies to make money.
I love you.*

Preface

For so long I have wanted to share my story. Thank you for being here. Thank you for taking the time to pick up this memoir.

The many polarizing topics that go through my mind needed a home, so I wrote this book. I also wanted to tell you my experience because there are a lot of stereotypes and preconceived ideas that people have about the adult industry that aren't true, and some that are. I wanted to help clarify those for inquiring minds and rebels like myself.

I hope you find yourself entertained, educated, and empowered by this tale. I love the idea that you might leave this story feeling differently than when you started reading it. I am hopeful to see a more inclusive world that views sex workers as equal members of society, porn as art, and performers as artists.

Introduction

Hello, my name is Rachel. I'm a thirty-four-year-old bisexual woman who lives on the mountainside in Topanga Canyon, California. I have lots of animals, including two potbellied pigs and two French bulldogs. I enjoy decorating and art. I have invested my adult life in being a sex worker. I am proud of the work that I have done, and I am also teetering on the verge of saying goodbye to it. I am so grateful for being able to work in this business for over a decade and for all the support I have been given. The sex industry will always have a special place in my heart. Whatever you may hear in this book is my truth and only my truth. I have changed many people's names to hide their identity and left certain people's names unadjusted for personal reasons. I want you to know that no matter how negative a story in here might be, it doesn't take away from the joy I have gotten out of the freedom of sex work.

"How did you get into porn?" has always been a question people ask me, so I figured I would tell you. Enjoy!

Drugs, Boobs, and Bunnies

I awoke in a drugged-up stupor, with double D–size breasts and a perfect little nose, though I couldn't see either due to the white bandages that covered my swollen body and bruised face. I was recovering at the W Hotel in chic-as-fuck West Beverly Hills, California, a luxurious hotel in a cute college town, right next to Hugh Hefner's old mansion and adjacent to my university at the time, UCLA. I was twenty-one years old, my father had just died, and I had spent over $20,000 of his life insurance money on plastic surgery. Even though I had received a couple hundred thousand dollars from his policy, I was in no mental state to fight for my multimillion-dollar trust fund that my evil stepmother was sitting on. My father had lost a battle with sarcoma (blood and tissue cancer) after two long years of fighting tooth and nail to survive. My last memory of him was when my stepmother pulled the plug on Christmas Day. Sure, he wasn't going to make it, but why she chose Christmas Day as his death day, I'll never know. I blasted the song "Last Resort" by Papa Roach as the realization sank in. My father was dead, forever. I couldn't believe it. So, I just sat there on the oversize sofa screaming the lyrics, "Cut my life into pieces, this is my last resort, suffocation, no breathing, don't give a fuck if . . ." as my stepsiblings stared at me in disbelief.

"Hide his art—take everything to storage!" my twisted step-mother scathingly whispered to her son. She didn't want me to have anything of my father's. That would become clear soon enough.

He had tried every solution: experimental procedures, expensive procedures; you name it, he tried it. He was a handsome man, an active man, and an overall Renaissance man. Everyone in Newport Beach, where he resided, wanted to be like him. After all, he had beautiful children, a picturesque home in a coveted private neighborhood, a yacht, a sailboat, a membership to the best country club in town, and a hot mistress on the side, all before age sixty-five. He spoiled me rotten, but not as much as his stepchildren, which I would grow to resent later on in life.

In preparation for surgery, I booked myself a lavish suite at the W Hotel, where I was going to recover in decadence and allow myself a glamorous mourning. I started by going full throttle, trusting Dr. Garth Fisher and Dr. Raj Kanodia to perfect my youthful body and face, perhaps to distract myself from what just happened. They changed the direction of my career for the better, opening many doors for me in an industry where your appearance is your ticket in. My whole life, I had been insecure about my nose. I was teased about it in middle school and in high school, and then I never felt fully confident with my profile when I started posing for sexy photos. I couldn't shake the memory of the house party where, before one of my first hookups, a handsome upper-classman had discussed my nose with his friend right in front of me, and his friend had commented, "She's pretty except for her nose!" tracing his own profile to demonstrate what he meant.

He was talking about my dorsal hump nose, where there was a bump in the center, noticeable when I turned to the side. I am not blaming my insecurity about my nose on the people who commented on it throughout my life, but it definitely didn't help. I was never the prettiest girl in high school, but I was always smart and popular. Growing up, my best friend, Clara, came from a famous Hollywood family, who would send us a limo every weekend to visit them in the hills of Los Angeles. Ted Field, a successful producer behind movies such as *FernGully* and *The Hand That Rocks the Cradle*, was her father. His many girlfriends were always Playmates and supermodels—they were stunning. I grew up idolizing them and the lifestyle they had curated for themselves. Ted had a close friend, Raj Kanodia, who also happened to be the best rhinoplasty surgeon in the world.

Fast-forward thirteen years later and I am doing my research at the *Playboy* Mansion, trying to find the best plastic surgeons, and all of sudden life comes full circle. Asking all my weekend girlfriends whom I should go to to get work done was easy; they all went to the same two surgeons, Fisher and Kanodia. It's a small world here in Southern California, and everyone knows everyone. The doctors gave me a discount for being one of Hef's girls—just another perk of the position.

Waking up from such a hard-core surgery is a blur. I was highly medicated when they rolled me out of the hospital in a wheelchair. I know my mother, Michelle, picked me up because the surgeon later told me what a delight she was. The way he said it immediately made me realize she had probably flirted with him; she flirts with everyone. I do not. I try my best to be professional so that people will not conflate my natural friendliness with flirtation. My mother and I have a love-hate relationship. I vividly recall wearing a forest-green True Religion sweat suit the morning of the big day, which I had purchased specifically for recovery. "You really don't have a stitch of makeup on, do you?" she passive-aggressively sneered. She always has made little comments to poke at me. After I woke up in my hotel suite, five of my closest friends from high school took turns visiting me during recovery. They brought me flowers and cards and acted like what I had done to myself was pretty intense.

"There's a huge elephant on my chest, just sitting here and weighing me down!" I kept reiterating that, and to this day the immense pressure of the imaginary yet painful elephant is clear in my memory. In a blurry haze, I asked one of my oldest friends, Nathan, if he could please fetch me my pain medication—and that is when we realized it was gone. In the guise of making sure I wouldn't become dependent on it; my mother snatched those fun little suckers right up for herself. Mother has been in and out of rehab a couple of times and is an addict. She is a wild and fun-loving person who struggles with depression and an affinity for Chardonnay and pain pills. Watching my mom's personality shift with drugs and alcohol while I was growing up is enough to make me gag at the smell of white wine.

Now with no medication and an elephant on my chest, what was I to do? I kept throwing up, over and over again, just hurling out the nothingness that was inside of me. This was my therapy. I went from my beloved father dying straight into what I thought would make me a happier, more confident person: plastic surgery.

"Are you okay?" Lacey shouted through the door in the bath-room as I barfed everywhere. I was obviously not okay. In so much pain I could hardly move, I was lucky to have my friends in and out of the hotel checking on me, even if my mom had taken off with my drugs. To this day my girlfriend Cindy tells the story of my recovery at parties and vows never to get work done because of it. I was a hot mess.

Within a week or two, I was back in my black Porsche Cayenne, which I had bought in cash, speeding around town. I got pulled over by a police officer for running a stop sign. I wheedled my way out of the ticket because I showed him my nose bandages and he felt bad for me. Shit, *I* felt bad for me; I was a mess and a half.

Today, it's been twelve years, many hours, and thousands of dollars of therapy later and I still haven't gotten over the death of my father. The best way I can describe the pain is that there's a wave that keeps hitting me, but the magnitude just feels a little less sudden with every hit. My therapist told me that would happen. Grieving the death of a parent is the worst pain I've ever felt. That following week, I was in class, bruises, bandages, and all. People stared, but no one dared to ask me why my face looked blue and wrapped. They probably just assumed it was plastic surgery; this is LA, after all. A weird part about death is that life goes on, even though your special person died; that seems cruel, doesn't it?

I had recently read the memoir *How to Make Love Like a Porn Star*, about Jenna Jameson, cowritten with Neil Strauss, and it had changed me. Great pieces of art will do that to you. They will excite you and tantalize you and move me, and that is exactly how I felt after reading this book. I recovered from plastic surgery by watching old porn movies in my plush hotel bed, renting *The New Devil in Miss Jones*, an erotic movie by Vivid Pictures, starring Jenna Jameson.

What appealed to me most was the glamour, beauty, and femininity that Jenna seemed to exude on film. There was also something masculine and strong coming through as I watched her brave performance. I loved the athleticism of the sex itself; it was like the best of the best competitors doing the most enjoyable thing imaginable. I thought that the mere concept—that she was monetizing her physical body as a brand—was the coolest thing in the world. I was already in the sex industry, but this genre seemed more appealing than the escort work I had been up to. I had always had a strong desire to entertain people. I was athletic, a businesswoman, and this job seemed like the right fit for me. I had watched documentaries about adult film stars while I was in high school and thought, *That looks like the greatest job ever.*

How could someone get paid for having sex on film and do it with so much grace? I wasn't fully aware that the movie was made in the golden age of porn. I also wasn't aware that the adult industry changes its business model every decade. DVDs and feature films would soon be on their way out. I related to the unbridled women in front of the camera, and I knew that I had to be one of them. I felt like I was meant to be a porn star. I was in a lot of pain in that hotel bed, but I had an epiphany about what I wanted my future to look like. The same way men idolize football players, I idolized Tera Patrick, Stormy Daniels, Carmen Electra, Jenna Jameson, Pamela Anderson, and so many other powerful and beautiful women.

Now all I had to do was dive into their world. But where would I start? The best way I can explain the feeling of knowing I was made to do something was that I couldn't imagine my life without being able to model nude. That was where it all began . . .

Don't Lose Your Towel
or Your Virginity

"Don't lose your towel or your virginity!" my mother yelled as she dropped me and my best friends off in her white 1979 Volkswagen convertible at one of the most exclusive beaches in all of Orange County, Emerald Bay. E-bay, as we called it, was the place to be and to be seen, especially when I was a freshman in high school trying to establish my social status. I grew up in the most privileged, beautiful beach town in SoCal, the charming Laguna Beach, in a 1920s cottage. My mother's home regularly graced the glossy pages of well-known magazines such as *House Beautiful* and *Cottage Living*, the OG highlight reel. With an ocean view from my balcony and a chic black Mercedes-Benz CLK convertible as my first car, I was fierce. On the outside looking in, I had it made in the shade. Appearances can be deceiving.

However, "the OC" isn't perfect. Far from it. My friends and peers opened up our lives for a legendary MTV reality show called *Laguna Beach* circa 2004 and showed those imperfections to the world. It was a show that would set the precedent for all reality-drama television to come. The show was the first of its kind, blurring the lines between reality and scripted television, not fully disclosing how realistic the events were and how much of them were contrived. Even before that, films and television had portrayed Orange County families living a lavish lifestyle of money and riches, juxtaposed with the hidden truth of deception, drugs, and an unstable home life. That story was a true story; that story was my story.

My father, Jules Arie Swimmer, had emigrated from Israel (which he still called Palestine) in 1951 to Toronto, Canada. Growing up in extreme poverty and fleeing from the aftermath of World War II, my father was a real rags-to-riches story. He went from sharing filthy bathwater with his siblings because his family didn't have enough money for clean water to bathe in to becoming a doctor, then a real estate developer, and eventually a multimillionaire and pillar of the Newport Beach community. Married three times, with six children, Jules was a boss. He had many luxury cars, a beautiful home in a private community called Shore Cliffs in Corona Del Mar, California, and a lot of nude photos of women around the house. He also had a serious girlfriend (who was also married) at his side in the hospital before he passed away. She even requested to attend his funeral, but that request was swiftly denied by his spouse at the time. In 2010, he had two phones: one for his lover and one for his wife. He was a great father in many ways but, at the same time, negligent in others. He kicked me out of his house when I was sixteen years old because he thought I was having sex with the boy I had invited over. I was not.

The subtle but pervasive sex shame came early for me. I have many fond memories of time with my father, from rollerblading down the Newport Peninsula to Caribbean vacations with the whole family. When I think of my dad, I think of the good. I only wish I had more time with him. The loss of my father hit me hard. The pain of his death has never gone away, but at least the pain has gotten less all-encompassing over the decade.

My mother is from West Covina, California. She grew up immersed in twelve years of Catholic school, getting hit with a ruler by nuns and all. She often brings up tales of her having to have worn a dunce cap and being punished for her sexuality—her white blouse that got her sent home from school for "tempting the boys." She has an aversion to religion because of it and has since become an atheist. She was sexually abused as a child by a neighbor and continues to suffer from that trauma. Her upbringing was far from the cushy lifestyle of the Orange County elite. Her father was instead a blue-collar truck driver and her mother a devout Catholic wife, who had five children and a small weekly allowance. When my uncle was just five years old, he shot and killed his best friend, a neighborhood boy, with my grandfather's rifle. No wonder my mom has always been so adamant and politically outspoken about gun control.

She got kicked out of the house as a teen, rebelling against her conservative parents and becoming a hippie. She purchased an orange VW van and grew waist-length straight blonde hair. She worked at Bob's Big Boy, Marie Callender's, and other restaurants, waiting tables to put herself through UCLA—all while living in Westwood and dating rock stars. To this day, she randomly brings up anecdotes about dating the lead singer and guitarist of the band Pablo Cruise and the drummer from the Tijuana Brass, and she speaks of her days of old like they were just yesterday. She reminds me to live in the moment and not cling so hard to the past. She was a babe, with green eyes, standing five-seven with perfectly straight teeth and a bunny-slope nose to boot.

She fell deeply in love with my already-married father while on a work trip in Toronto. My father and his friend literally chased my mom into a parking structure, where his friend proceeded to ask her out. She kindly declined and insisted my father take her out instead. He claimed to be in an open relationship, and since it was the seventies, that was believable—but unfortunately inaccurately represented. My dad's first wife didn't mean for him to meet some blonde shiksa who flashed her boobs at cars and then run off into the sunset with her, but he did. He was a cute lifeguard-turned-dentist, and my mom was just crazy about him. His fashionable appearance and Jewish ethnicity drew her in. He was fifteen years her senior, and she fell head over heels in love with him. He wore big fur coats and got his nails done; he was a progressive man. They worked together building his dentistry practice. He defaulted on his Canadian taxes and they road-tripped right down to Laguna Beach, California, leaving his two children, my half siblings, behind. Their impression of our father was never quite as dreamy as mine. He was ready to start his new life with my mom, and that's precisely what he did.

My mom married twice, once for love and once for the baby, my little sister. She had two children and became a well-known interior designer, furnishing luxury homes, commercial real estate, and our own beautiful cottage. My mom's second marriage was to the district attorney of Orange County. Ronald was a true terror to live with; he was strict, particular, and especially controlling over my mother. I remember the smell of red wine on his gray mustache and him playing "American Pie" on his guitar by the fireplace. He was a sweet dad who sang loving country songs to us, but he had an aggressive temper that you might not imagine a prosecutor to have.

He had a strict budget for a poor man, let alone a wealthy man, which he was. He wouldn't allow us to use the air-conditioning in his mansion by the sea, so when he was away at work, my mother used to blast it and open all the windows. When he got home from work, he expected us to eat as a family. We had specific chairs we were supposed to sit in, and if we moved from those chairs, we would be scorned and screamed at. I have a vague memory of wanting to try my baby sister's food one evening and throwing it up, right into my plate. Ronald said, "You wanted to try the food, now you have to eat what's on your plate." He was full of anger, and I ended many meals at our home in tears. He ran a tight ship and was constantly on edge; this didn't sit well with my mother. She moved us out of his house; my little sister was under a year old. Oddly enough, my mom moved us into her ob-gyn's home.

Once we moved into the doctor's beautiful house on Lido Island, it was clear he was madly in love with her. He would take stunning photographs of us. In his free time, he was a part-time archaeologist and wildlife photographer. Dr. Green wanted a third child in the family, but my mom felt like two babies from two different men was all that she could possibly handle. Three children from three different men would make her a floozy. So, she ran, far from him and back to retreat to our cottage by the ocean. I often wonder what happened to Dr. Green and whom he ended up marrying. I wonder where he is now and if perhaps my mom missed out on her happy ending. I just friended him on Facebook.

My mom may not have been fiscally responsible, but she was bold. She was always over-the-top and always thought she was in the right. She spoiled my sister and me financially, gifting us with Tiffany & Co. necklaces and matching bracelets in our Easter egg baskets. She took us on semiregular shopping sprees, and we had more trinkets and goodies than most of our very wealthy peers. My mom loved spending money, especially our fathers' child support checks—although she frequently complained that they weren't enough, they weren't on time, and that she hated Ronald specifically. All the big no-nos of parenting. Since my sister and I are half siblings and my mother favored my father, I was treated a little differently.

She was meant to live a more luxurious life, but her budgeting—or lack thereof—got her in trouble. And her anger when the child support checks ended was indescribable. Selling both of our homes and renting a small apartment to survive was her game plan. That was one of the trickiest parts of divorce; often, the woman had majority custody and was mostly living off the child support, raising her children and doing "women's work" for eighteen or so years. Then, all of a sudden she's fifty-plus years old and supposed to somehow join the modern workforce. I can only imagine how confusing that would be and how very difficult the burden. Our mom's house was the "cool house." She would let my girlfriends and me throw parties; we could have boys spend the night, smoke weed, and drink liquor. She just turned the other cheek and really thought we were safer at home than doing it somewhere else. Most of all, it made her "fun" and well-liked, which she really thrived on—typical narcissist behavior.

"What the fuck is wrong with you? Never have children, it ruined my life, you little FUCK! You ungrateful brats! Fuck you, fuck you, Rachel!" my mom yelled throughout my childhood, reiterating the message in different words. She verbally abused me and made home life extremely unstable, to the point I wanted to be anywhere but there. I never knew what I was walking into or what mood my mom was going to be in. As an alcoholic, she was constantly speaking to us in a way that a hateful owner would speak to his abused dog, like she wished we didn't exist. My father was my rock, but my mother raised me. She made sure I had the best of everything, but she was also insane. I love her dearly, and at the same time I loathe her. She has been a huge influence on my life and my character. Michelle is a legend among my friends in Laguna, especially because she let us party at her house. But for me she had this dark side that was reminiscent of Dr. Jekyll and Mr. Hyde. Although still alive, she suffers from health conditions that make it almost impossible for her to function and be an active part of my life, so every day I mourn the loss of what was.

I remember the powdered-sugar strawberries she used to serve us, the chocolate chip cookies she used to bake for us, and the snack drawer she used to stock for us. Dancing with her in our living room to Madonna, her encouraging words, her gorgeous smile and reading to us every chance she got when we were kids those are the memories I want to remember.

Incense always reminds me of when I was eleven years old, doing yoga next door to the head shop in Laguna Beach. My girlfriend's mom, Pam, would take us into an incense-infused yoga studio atop the grungy Mexican food restaurant Taco Loco to practice our meditation and poses. I was flexible, thin, and could throw my legs over my head like it was nothing. I could stand on my head and bend in every which way. I loved the art. I loved the Hindu figurines and artwork of elephants and women with many arms. I thought that henna tattoos and seventies culture was so fascinating. I was a wannabe hippie trapped in a middle schooler's body. "Look at those curves!" the female yoga teacher announced to our little classroom, because I would wear midriff-baring clothing and low-rise, stretchy pants. My body developed quicker than most girls' in my grade, and it was noticeable. My hips were curvaceous and my boobs swollen and perky. It was the typical commentary about my body that I was just used to receiving and thought was flattering; I had no idea how inappropriate these adults' comments about my child's body were. Furthermore, my mom would perpetuate that excitement and flattery around my body, constantly telling me to "Come downstairs to show my friends your tight little ass! Go on, turn around honey! Isn't she perfect!" she would tell her girlfriends as she patted my ass. She even went as far as to nicknaming me "Ritzy Titsy," because I developed breasts so early. I know it's cringeworthy. I look back and often think, "She groomed me to be a porn star."

When I was a young girl, I ran around my house naked. AOL

dial-up had just become popular amongst my peers, and I, like so many underaged teens, had found the trove of internet porn on illegal tube sites. "I've got porn star boobs. I've got porn star boobs!" I would scream. I was not discouraged in doing so—my mother allowed me to express myself in any way I saw fit. The Spice Girls were my role models, and I, along with the rest of world, was absolutely in love with their femininity and sexuality. I dressed up like them. I wore thigh-high white socks and big platform heels like them. I ran for fifth-grade class president and lost to a boy named Patrick. I was confident, popular, constantly getting in trouble for "dress code violations" and too much eye makeup. In all fairness, my mom drew black eyeliner on my sweet little face and forgot to help me remove it at the end of cotillion, an etiquette class I was enrolled in at ten years old. My teacher humiliated me in front of the entire classroom, asking, "Are you wearing eyeliner?" and then holding a meeting about the issue after school. I was shamed.

I developed large breasts at age twelve. I was always curious about sex; I remember masturbating when I was in elementary school, like so many kids do. But I got in devastating trouble with a girl named Annie because her parents caught us humping pillows. I had learned how to from a girl next door. They were furious, mostly because we were both girls: lesbians, they thought. They screamed and shouted at us about how wrong what we were doing was. This shame about lesbian sex started young. Ever since then, I had been on edge, thinking I was a lesbian and how awful that would make me. After all, I didn't personally know any lesbians growing up, even in the LBGTQ-proud town of Laguna Beach. Like many other bisexual girls, I didn't have anyone that represented me in media to identify with. My mother used to refer to the two women across the street as dykes, so I really didn't have a healthy outlook on what being gay would look like for me. I just knew it was something I couldn't be and that it was wrong.

In third grade, my favorite movie was *Clueless*. My mom let me watch movies that were unsuitable for my age—"As long as they don't have violence in them!" she would say. Sex in film was okay to watch, she said, because it was "natural"—which in hindsight is inaccurate. Even if the sex on television was portrayed in an authentic way, I was not media-literate. I don't recall having a thorough sex education. One evening, my girlfriend Bettie and I lay in my downstairs-bedroom bunk beds as we watched the film on my television; I had the top, she had the bottom. I loved watching Alicia Silverstone play the role of Cher. With her bouncy blonde locks, stunning face, and girly banter, she was everything I hoped to become. I looked up to her with envy and desire, wishing my dad had a mansion in Bel Air and I had a custom closet where I could pick out clothing with the touch of a button.

If you remember, there's a scene where Cher is trying to impress her closeted gay friend by being sexy because she thinks he's straight. She rolls off her bed and onto the floor. I was too embarrassed to admit it at the time, but in imitating Cher, I rolled off my bed and consequently cracked open my chin. I must have misgauged the comforter's width, or maybe at eight years old I didn't think falling six feet onto the hardwood floors would be painful. Down, down I went, tumbling onto my face. I fell, "splat!" and my chin split open on our oak floor like an egg dropping from a second-story building. Red blood splattered everywhere onto the wood. My bone showed right through the thin skin layer of my face, and I could feel my exposed jaw as I touched my chin. I ran into the bathroom to peer into the antique mirror—I had never seen anything this gruesome in real life. I ran with all my might to get upstairs and notify my mom, who was talking on the phone. "Oh God, Kathy, I've got to go!" she said in a very serious voice, clearly terrified for me.

She rushed me to the emergency room, throwing my girlfriend and my sister into the car to accompany us. I was told that I would need stitches, and although my situation was serious, I kept trying to push off that medical procedure for fear of pain. I've never liked physical pain. Fifteen stitches to my chin and a terrible scar twenty-five years later, I still must remind myself to put out my hands for protection when I fall or trip in order to protect my face. I guess I don't have that innate reflex. But I sure knew that telling people just how I fell off the bed that night was going to paint me in an unsavory light, so up until I was in my twenties, I lied about how I fell off the bunk that evening. It was as if even in elementary school I knew that saying "I was just trying to be sexy like Cher in *Clueless*" was going to bring me shame and embarrassment.

One vote, two vote, three vote . . . four. How many times is too many? Will the upperclassman see that the handwriting is all the same? I wondered at fourteen as I cast "Rachel" for homecoming queen into the bucket. I didn't think much of it at the time, but rigging an election my freshman year was certainly questionable, at least morally. I must have known I wasn't getting the popular vote, and I really wanted that title—no, I *needed* that title. I'm not sure anyone saw me, but I feel like the upperclassmen knew as they announced, "And the homecoming queen is Rachel Swimmer," over the loudspeaker on the football field. I even got a few sneers and glances from them as I stumbled down the steps in my trendy six-inch platforms to fraudulently board the float that was for the homecoming court. A girl can dream, can't she? I just wanted so badly to fit in, to be the cool kid, and of course to be homecoming queen. This stunt wasn't the first of its kind. In the seventh grade, I went as far as claiming to my peers that I was invited to someone's slumber party when I wasn't. Ironically, I still have mutual friends with the girl I claimed invited me, and I still think of it every time I see her. I just wanted to belong. Fitting in has always mattered to me, to some degree or another. Being different, as a young bisexual girl, made me feel insecure.

Daddy's Little Girl

I often felt othered, especially spending time at my father's home with his newer family and my stepsiblings, who didn't treat me like a sister. All three of them shared the same biological parents and really stuck together. I always wondered what that feeling of belongingness felt like as I had no full siblings of my own.

What was life at my dad's house like? Let me tell you about Darcy, their mother . . . If you thought you knew determination, cunningness, and manipulation, you hadn't met my stepmother, Darcy. She knew what she wanted and how to get it. She had my father wrapped around her finger. Whatever Darcy said went. She tried her best to fulfill the role of doting stepmother, but her attempts fell short, and she soon became an evil stepmonster. She loved her liquor, and she loved her hard-core narcotics. She put my older stepsister, Daphne, on a pedestal fit for a queen. She would let Daphne go shopping to her heart's desire, enrolled her in private singing classes, and obviously favored her because, after all, she was her real daughter. "Darcy, the Wicked Witch," my mom and I used to call her. Horrifying stepmothers are a thing of fiction, movies, and fairy tales, but my real-life stepmom was a true cliché. She was powerful, thin, blue-eyed, and beautiful, much like my actual mother. When she met my dad, she was a stunning blonde with sharp European features, but unlike my mother, she was my father's third wife and brought children into their marriage who took priority over his actual kids.

Darcy had two sides, a sweet, childlike side that she would use to manipulate me, and a dark side that she reserved for people closest to her and blue-collar workers. She was truly a force to be reckoned with. I owe a lot of my determination to this woman, but her disposition was insane and unpredictable. Alcoholism and drug addiction riddled her throughout her life, woven in and out of my memory from a young age. The smell of hard liquor reminds me of her. She would hide bottles of vodka everywhere—throughout the house, behind plants, in the laundry area—as if we couldn't see them.

Darcy was intense—so intense that she tried to commit suicide by locking herself in our garage and turning on all the vehicles, in hopes to die from carbon monoxide poisoning. She was arrested for drunk driving and sent to rehabs and facilities a multitude of times. It was the norm with her. She battled breast cancer for well over a decade and went through round after round of chemo, losing all her hair, throwing up nonstop, and almost surviving. The stench of drugs and barf reeked throughout the home. My father had a long-lasting love affair with a woman in a nearby community, Samantha, whom Darcy knew all about. It is my belief that she used drugs and attempted suicide to cope with the pain of that ongoing relationship, among other things. She had a lighter side, though; I'll never forget when she handed me my dad's checkbook in order to make him buy me a rare brindle-black French bulldog puppy named Stitch. My dad had agreed to simply look at puppies with me at a breeder nearby. Darcy knew he was going to "forget his check book at home," so she gave it to me. Then, at the end of the visit, my dad tried using his line—"Oh, we need to go home and think about it!" and I whipped that checkbook out, just like I had been trained to. I sealed the deal with, "Dad, you just spent $10,000 on a toilet seat for your yacht, so this is the least you could do!" Darcy had given me this intel and line to say dramatically. She made life more fun, some of the time.

She treated me like Cinderella, and her children never quite accepted me as part of their family. I was always the "fourth" wheel, and I felt like I was intruding on my dad's new world even though he remarried when I was only three years old. Darcy hung photos of her children above my father's home office and left me out, as if I didn't exist. I was the black sheep of the family, and I could never be quite as loved as her kids.

First Loves Die Hard

The perfect temperature, eighty degrees with an ocean breeze, and everyone's excited because school's finally out and long beach days are in full session: that was the constant feeling of summer in our small town. The summer of 2005 was when I met Jeff, my high school sweetheart. He was my everything, my savior from a fucked-up family, my light. He was the world to me and my first true love. We met at the beach and never left each other's sides after that. He was a nerd, but his wealth and charm allowed for him to fit in to my clique. Smarter and kinder than any boy I had ever met, Jeff was my soul mate.

Laguna is divided into two parts, No Lag and So Lag. No Lag (North Laguna) is home to a typically wealthier and snobbier group of kids from families that reflect those attributes. I lived in No Lag with my mom most of the time, although not in a gated community. My father lived in a private neighborhood in Newport Beach, which I visited on Wednesdays and every other weekend. I spent the majority of my time at my liberal mom's house, right outside of Emerald Bay, the most coveted enclave to grow up in as a young teen. All the cute boys lived there, and the association had its own private beach with tons of fun family-friendly activities. It was prestigious yet cool to be a part of E-bay. Luckily, lots of my friends lived there, as did the boys I hooked up with. I always yearned to be part of that world; it felt like I was always so close but so far away. It felt like the badge was being waved in my face, literally feet away from me, teasing me in but never letting me stay inside the green, spiked gates, in one of the "perfect" families with married parents. All the parents were married in E-bay . . . while my mom was a single mom through and through. Our house was the "fun" house, where we could eat whatever, smoke whatever, party whenever, play Dance Dance Revolution whenever, but it wasn't stable. Ironically, Jeff lived in E-bay, but I didn't quite care for his dad, so I avoided his family gatherings.

So Lag was like a Southern Californian version of *Blue Crush*. Surfing, skim boarding, and smoking weed was part of the regular weekday schedule for the kids in South Laguna. I loved South Laguna. The parents seemed more relaxed, more hippie-like, the way Laguna was supposed to be. Laguna has a deep culture of progressive liberal artists, many of them LGBTQ, who flocked to the area and created an eccentric community full of beauty and art. Then Orange County as a whole became more conservative and Laguna's diverse history began to wash away, turning into a packed tourist destination.

You know you're in the OC when the freeways widen and there is plenty of space to park, unlike in crowded Los Angeles. I refer to it as "the red state," because it really does feel like its own separate state. People are old-timey, and it's like going back a couple of decades. The culture is also deeply racist. People often look the same. I can spot an Orange County native from a mile away. It's fun for the weekend, but I don't think I would move back there permanently.

We grew up fast, regardless of the side of town, and when I say fast, I mean it. I was smoking weed at twelve years old. I got my belly button pierced in seventh grade after my father persuaded me to sign a waiver saying I would stay sexually abstinent and drug-free in high school in exchange. This agreement was like a contract version of a purity ring. I had to promise to stay a virgin through senior year and stay away from narcotics—promises I couldn't keep. There was some creepy clause in there about heavy petting being an exception, which is such a boundary overstep that I can't believe my dad came up with it, but go figure. I signed it. I was experimenting with blow jobs on my gay bestie (I didn't know he was gay at the time), all in that same year. Ironically, he came from the most Christian family, and his older brother walked in on us as I attempted the act.

Seventh grade was a killer. Those were really the days when I rebelled. I had no rules at home with Michelle, so honestly, it's a miracle I survived. My mom never gave my little sister and me a curfew. There were no rules about sex in her house; she preferred we party at home so we didn't get into trouble elsewhere. When I hit fifteen years of age, my mom was picking me up at 3:00 a.m. at parties in the canyon, a seedier little area in Laguna where other parents with no rules let us party. And party we did. We would experiment with our parents' prescription medication, alcohol, sex—you name it. It was just the culture to be able to do so, every year getting progressively more extreme.

My freshman year in high school, my mom met another man, an alcoholic with white hair, whom I often mistook for someone experiencing homelessness when I saw him walking down the street. We didn't get along; although I was happy my mother had found love again, I couldn't stand this guy. Having stepparents or accepting my parent's new partners was always hard for me, but this old guy who looked like Santa and drank like a sailor? My mom could do better. He let my peers and me use his house to throw ragers, as we called the parties, and then would scream and yell at us when they got out of control. Of course they were going to get out of control—we were fourteen years old and hosting older kids for booze and weed. Once he slammed the garage door with me inside the garage and started regularly yelling at me, I knew I had to leave Laguna. I couldn't cohabitate with this asshole.

I begged to be shipped off to boarding school. I pitched my

father the reasons I should go and the advantages an elite boarding school would offer us, like better preparation for an Ivy League college. He eventually obliged, shelling out the $50,000 a year it would cost me to study in Pebble Beach, California, at a prep school called Robert Lewis Stevenson. At RLS, I boarded in the dorm rooms with a girl from Hong Kong named Vanessa. She was sweet, smart, and worked into the wee hours to earn great grades. She also played trumpet, ran track, and managed to have a boyfriend. I was busy partying, doing cocaine, making out with boys, and trying to fit in. I used this escape from home to grow up quicker and have fun. I let my grades slip and was not asked back the following year. I wonder if they saw me doing a line or two in the forest on a tree trunk, or if it was the make-out sessions on the golf course that had them uninterested in my reenrollment. A lot has changed since then, but I still identify as a rebel.

The Virgin Whore

Why is it that when a woman "loses" her virginity, she experiences a loss and a man "gains" the virginity of that woman? Is the woman not gaining an experience herself? Is it the mere fact a man has a penis that enters and a woman has a vagina that receives that makes it so? If that is the case and a woman is the receiver, shouldn't she, too, be getting something? Why is there so much shame, pressure, and buildup around virginity?

I was fifteen years old and attending Robert Lewis Stevenson when I was asked to prom by a cute Russian guy named Andrew. I accepted. Andrew was over six feet tall, blond, blue-eyed, and attractive. He didn't go to RLS but attended a public high school about fifteen minutes away in Pacific Grove. He was a great golfer who ended up attending Harvard University, playing on their golf team. He had a sweet family whom I met before the dance. His mom took photos of us by their mantel, and he bought me a pretty pink-and-white corsage. Andrew had a shitty red Mazda that he drove us to and from prom in. The dance was insignificant compared to the afterparty.

I don't recall us talking about a plan to have sex that night. Andrew offered me a vodka–and–orange juice concoction, and I eagerly accepted it. We were alone. Then we started making out and getting naked in someone's living room. He whipped out his penis. It was large and honestly looked intimidating. There was no real talk about the deed, I certainly wanted to try to engage, but Andrew went to push his tip into my vagina—with no success. It wasn't going to go in, no questions asked. We didn't even know what lubricant was, and I wasn't educated about having to be wet or turned on for me to able to enjoy anything. So, it literally was just the tip and nothing more. I didn't lose my virginity that night (at least not in my mind, but that didn't stop Andrew from telling his friends), but we did sleep in his smelly car, pulled over on the side of a road in a neighborhood close by Pacific Grove. His parents wouldn't have been cool with me sleeping over, and he couldn't drop me off past curfew in my dorm room at RLS, so we roughed it that night and cuddled up with one another. Did Andrew think he took my virginity? He certainly told people so. I knew for certain that I was still a virgin, but I still told my girlfriends back in Laguna what happened that night, maybe for clout, maybe to seem like I was mature.

The second time I lost my virginity, it was less innocent. I was still fifteen years old, but it was summer, and I was home in Orange County. On this particular day, the house party was on my dad's block in Corona Del Mar at the home of a boy named Jordan. His parents must have been gone, because this was a huge celebration. I reunited with my ex-boyfriend who at the time was a drug dealer and someone who used to slip his elderly parents Xanax bars to knock them out and trash their home for parties. He would brag to me and my girlfriends about it. He raided my mother's bathroom for her Ambien and stole large bottles of vodka from local grocery stores, hiding them in his pant legs—he was trouble. The first time I met his mother, she showed me her schnauzer dogs and the braces she had put on them illegally. She was training them to compete in dog pageants, and if she was going to win, she needed their teeth straight. I was alarmed.

One night while I was visiting his house, he asked if I wanted any Xanax, Ambien, or some drug I can't clearly recall, and I accepted. I took the pill and slowly began to drift into a sleepy place. I vaguely remember undressing. I have a foggy recollection of him having sex with me while I was almost passed out. I am not positive what happened. When I woke up he was gone . . . This would have surely been questionable by today's standards, but back in 2005 it didn't feel like that. I had never even heard of the word *consent*. The whole memory is still very blurry.

Finally, when Jeff became my high school sweetheart, I consciously and coherently "lost" my virginity to him in my own cozy bedroom. He came in his pants before he even took them off. I told you he was a dork. It was true love.

Laguna Beach Season 3: The Season No One Remembers

I was turning sixteen years old, and I wanted everyone to know. My stepmother, Darcy, offered to throw my big bash. She took me to an exclusive party planner's warehouse in Costa Mesa and paid for me to be able to design the exact setup. She rented out the Hotel Laguna and let me create my own Barbie-themed invites. I picked out pastel beaded bracelets that each recipient had to show the bouncers at the door and a decadent, three-tiered pink cake with Barbie popping out of the top—the cake formed her dress. My favorite parts of the party were the multiple go-go dancers who stood atop platforms in skimpy outfits to entertain the high schoolers.

My party was the talk of Laguna Beach High, and everyone wanted an invite. I felt like a princess. I got a Mandalay dress that Paris Hilton also had; it was black silk, hand-embroidered with shiny gold beads that highlighted my teen breasts, and cost well over a grand. My mom threatened, "You better not gain a pound—this is the type of dress that will really show it!" as I tried on gowns at Novecento in Crystal Cove, an ocean-view shopping center. I got my hair and makeup done at MAC Cosmetics in the mall, because that was the place to go in 2006. I was ready to shine. My party was packed and was as over-the-top as a nice wedding. Friends and peers sprawled out on cabanas throughout the large banquet hall overlooking the ocean, helping themselves to the catered food. All of us danced up against one another, freak dancing in the dimly lit room with the DJ blasting Ja Rule and the Ying Yang Twins over the loudspeakers. "TO the window . . . to the wall . . . 'til the sweat drip down my balls." This was just one of the moments that I cherish and credit Darcy for. Although she was jealous of the relationship I had with my father, she could be overwhelmingly kind at times. I just never knew which side to expect. Was she going to ask me "Did you wear that outfit shopping with your father?" with distain in her voice or was she going to give me a hug? It was always a surprise. It was as if both my mom and my stepmother were resentful of me.

Growing up in Laguna is like growing up in Disneyland—it's a fantasy with some spooky rides, until you leave the Magic Kingdom, and then nothing can quite live up to it ever again. When I was sixteen years old, I was cast on a first-of-its-kind reality/drama television series called *Laguna Beach: The Real Orange County*, which aired on MTV. For those of you who aren't familiar with the show, it was a spin-off of *The O.C.*, a scripted series about teen life in Orange County. It was my absolute favorite show, and my friends and I held watch parties every

Thursday when it aired. Nothing beat Marissa Cooper and Summer Roberts (the lead characters) drinking their lattes, losing their virginities, and engaging in inappropriate behavior. What made the experience different for me and my cronies was that we were actually living it.

MTV came to Laguna Beach years before I was ever cast on the show. I was at Robert Lewis Stevenson, my prep school, when MTV cast the first season. It felt surreal to watch my hometown peers live on television in the common room. It made me feel nostalgic for home and the people I had grown up with. It also made me feel a little envious of their being cast on a hit television show.

I was not invited back to RLS, because my grades had dropped. I had recently returned to Laguna after completing my sophomore year away and was excited to see all my friends. I had a license to drive, and I blasted gangsta rap as I picked up my clique for outings in my shiny convertible. It was a Friday morning, and MTV was on campus. We all knew why they were there . . . they were casting season three of *Laguna Beach*, and I was going to be on it. Some things are just preordained. There was some sort of suggestion box that you could either enter yourself into or suggest others for. I remember my girlfriends and I leaving our info inside of it. Previous cast members were also asked to refer or recommend other people in the grade below them for the show, or at least that's what the casting director told us.

The only interview we had was one that was done in an office building in Laguna, where we sat on a literal casting couch and were asked about the drama we had with other people, how comfortable we were being filmed, and our friendship history with all the other "cool" girls on campus. Our group was cast right away. We were drama, or at least we knew that's what they were looking for.

"Would you like to be a cast member on the *Laguna Beach* show?" said Cara, our future producer. Oh my god, did I ever. Forget the pay, which was barely anything, a whopping $2,500 in total—we were going to be famous! We were going be on camera for all the world to see . . . *What teen wouldn't want that?* I thought. In reality, we were being taken advantage of financially, and in retrospect, we were too young to be making such life-changing decisions. How can you consent to exposing yourself on international television at the ripe age of sixteen? You can't. But my parents said it was okay because I wanted to do it so badly, and thus I was a cast member. There was no pushback, because as far as they could tell, there was no downside. Everyone from season one appeared to be thriving.

The director would call us the week before to plan out what events, locations, or ideas they had for filming. But unlike a purely scripted show, they let us take the lead most of the time. Because we had already seen the show for two years straight, we also had become less organic than previous cast members. We knew what the viewers wanted, so we were more contrived and attempted to live up to the big stars who came before us. The roles we had been cast in glorified us on campus among our peers. From our high school principal, who once pulled us out of class for a photo op to our classmates, who looked up to us—or down on us—we were the talk of the town. Our little village had always been a touristy destination, but after the show, it became the premiere place to visit. People from all over the world started to flock to our artist community.

Many people expected one thing and got another. The show portrayed us as rich kids, full of drama and growing up way too fast along the coast of Southern California. What they didn't capture was the real family life going on behind the scenes, the kids who didn't have as much money as their peers, the artisan community that was filled with LGBTQ people and hippies . . . but you can't blame the producers, either. After all, how could any camera crew capture that? And would that have even been a hit television show? The producers knew what their audience wanted, and they gave it to them. None of our parents were going to let a full-blown reality show happen within our homes during mundane, normal hours. We filmed on the weekends because we were minors and had school during the week. The shoot days were always planned in advance. There were some laws in place to protect our education and youth, but looking back, the whole thing seems unethical.

I got a call from Cara. "Rachel, do you think your dad will let us film you girls on his yacht this weekend?"

"Yes! Yes! That sounds awesome, I'll call him right now," I squealed with delight. I was ecstatic—I thought that maybe I would be a main character. After all, we'd filmed at my mom's house a couple of times. They filmed me while I asked an older boy to the winter formal by trashing his car with streamers. They had also filmed us shopping at South Coast Plaza, where I felt like I was the nucleus. . . . There was a chance.

The main characters were the focus of the show, while the friends were the buddies on the side. MTV didn't tell the cast who was going to be a main character and who was going to be a supporting character. We all filmed the same amount, so it was sometimes confusing. Looking back, I had rose-colored lenses on, because I wanted so badly to be a focal character.

Moments later I got the message that we would be filming instead on Bettie's dad's yacht, in a harbor not as nice as the one at the country club where my father docked his boat. I'll never know if Bettie called to change the location or if the producers did, but either way, I was devastated. These were superficial and trivial perils I faced on a weekly basis. This shouldn't have ever been on a high schooler's agenda. Who has the bigger yacht? Whose parents live in the biggest home? Who at school is the prettiest? At least, we shouldn't have faced those questions for a bunch of strangers to be entertained by. Did I mention we never got any residuals? Years later, I lied about this to peers out of sheer embarrassment. There was never a way to monetize the work we had done after we had done it. It was all up to chance, whether or not the show made each person famous. Not one actor/reality star in our season left with a real brand for themselves because of the show—at least not in the way that actors from seasons one and two did. With the money I earned, I bought myself a flat-screen television and spent the rest on food and clothing.

Looking back, I am utterly shocked that MTV allowed our red Solo cups full of alcohol on the air. As if anyone thought we were drinking soda. Can you imagine, sixteen-year-olds going to parties, getting miked up, and getting hammered filming a television show for the world to see? Our director, Kristina, would often ask us to repeat lines we'd said organically, even suggest things for us to talk about in order to control the narrative. It was a unique way of blending real life with an augmented, camera-ready reality. It had never been done.

We were given promotional items from all the local brands and surf shops that carried Billabong, Ugg, Roxy (she was a real person at our school, a couple grades older than us, and her dad named the brand after her). We got to do special promo shoots in our bikinis, interview prep in Los Angeles, and were treated like mini celebrities. The whole experience was enchanting. The catch was no one was told who the main characters were until the show wrapped, meaning we had to show up to set every shoot and give MTV our all, even if we were just going to be portrayed as some sidekick character. Guess what I became? "Rachel, Bettie's friend," for the entire season. I was wrecked. Was it because I wasn't pretty enough? Wealthy enough? It really messed with my self-esteem. That's the thing about being in the professional spotlight at an early age: your sense of self is completely tested. Are you some loser because you're just someone's friend? Why wasn't I a star character? I couldn't tell you. I can tell you what I told everyone: "Oh, my boyfriend comes from a conservative family, and because he can't be filmed, MTV doesn't want to make me a lead. Because love interests are the heart of the show. . . . " There was truth to this storyline, but I could feel my sense of self diminishing. The craziest part is that we all got paid the same and filmed the same, but about halfway through filming you could see whom the director would focus on. It wasn't Bettie's fault she was a born entertainer. I just wanted to be one, too!

The meaner you acted in front of the cameras, the more likely your scene was to air. That was the system MTV encouraged. One day while filming, I felt the urge to talk badly about a fellow cast member, Cindy, and contribute negatively to the shit-talking conversation. "Ew, who does she think she is? She doesn't even go to our school," I chimed in when her name came up in conversation surrounding the excitement of prom. I cringed after saying it. I knew that my voice was often ignored, but it wouldn't be then. Shortly after that episode aired, I got a call from our mutual friend on the show, telling me, "Cindy watched the episode and it hurt her feelings. . . . "

My heart sank. Was I ruining relationships that I had built my whole life, over some stupid reality television show that I was only a supporting character on? Yes, I was. When you're sixteen years old, you don't realize the long-term consequences of being broadcast on national television. Despite this, our friendship recovered, and just last year, I went to her baby shower. This type of anxiety around friendships and the limelight was a constant part of shooting. The show gave us a reason to showcase our most salacious selves. Even as teens we knew what sold, and that was drama. The people love drama.

In my family, college was never just an option. It was just a mandatory prerequisite of life. You go to college after high school, period. That said, I needed great grades in high school to get into a respected university. I've always been able to get high marks without trying very hard, but when my priorities shifted in high school to boys, partying, and securing a role on *Laguna Beach*, I gradually stopped caring about getting perfect scores in school. However, when college application time came around, I was devastated to learn I didn't have the grades to get into my family's alma mater, UCLA—or any prestigious university, for that matter. I had only gotten into a few backup schools that I never really wanted to go to in the first place. I had even forced my parents to take me into a private college counselor's office to help me secure a spot at an elite institution. The counselor sat down with my dad, my mom, and me, making it clear that we didn't need his services. Instead, what we needed was *family* counseling. Which was true. I had been in individual therapy from a young age, but I wasn't the problem—they were, and neither party was willing to admit it. I yearned for a stable, "normal" family.

Are You My Daddy?

"Your dad is not your dad! I'm your sister . . . my dad is your dad!" my cousin Laura yelled over the upbeat party music in the elegant ballroom of the Balboa Bay Country Club—hardly the place to air this dirty laundry. We were celebrating my dad's fiftieth birthday with a glamorous soiree.

Stumped and confused, I responded, "What do you mean?" I had no clue what she was talking about.

"Oh, your mom used my dad's sperm to have you, at a sperm bank . . . Go check for yourself! You're not related to your dad, at least not biologically." I just continued to dance and mingle and process this information. I had always thought Laura was a quack, so I didn't want to jump to any conclusions, but was it true? Was my father really my uncle Arnold? *I sure hope not*, I thought. Arnold was unattractive inside and out and constantly reeked of cigarette smoke—not exactly someone you would want as your father. He gave creep. I had no context about what this meant, so I chose to table the discussion for later.

"Mom, was I created in a lab?" I asked nonchalantly a few days after this bomb was dropped on me. Then there came a long pause and a look of annoyance. She had been caught in her own lie and didn't feel like getting into the nitty-gritty details.

"Why does it matter? Your dad and I really wanted to have you, but he had a vasectomy at a time when they were irreversible," my mom said. She has never been very motherly or empathic, so her response and aversion toward my questioning was no surprise, but it hurt nonetheless.

"Mom, is Uncle Arnold my sperm donor?" I asked. She quickly denied anything of the sort. She admitted that I was the product of a sperm donor. She said she had hand-selected a donor who looked like my father who raised me. That the donor was a healthy, brilliant medical student. This was such a cheesy story-line that I felt as though I was once again in a soapy drama. But no, this was just another day in my life as an Orange County teen. "I fucking hate my life; I'm going to kill myself!" I wailed in the bathroom as I processed this information more clearly. I never imagined that I would find out that the dad who raised me wasn't even my dad at all.

"You're not my real dad," I screamed as I shut myself in my stepsister's bedroom closet at my dad's house. Like my mom, he seemed insensitive and dismissive of my anger over the situation. My parents seemed ticked off that they had to have this conversation with me at all. It was clear as day that they were never planning to let me in on their heretical little secret. I had been created in a doctor's office using a random man's sperm.

"Why does it matter? I've always been a good dad to you," my father said matter-of-factly, as if once again this was about him and not about my broken heart. My parents never validating my feelings as a child took an enormous emotional toll on me.

Once I got a grip on the fact that my parents had wanted to create me so badly that they went to extreme measures in doing so, I was less angry. Undergoing IUI (intrauterine insemination) treatments with a viable sperm donor is a feat, physically, financially, and mentally. I tried my best to be grateful and move on from the trauma. I placed the knowledge in the back of my mind, where it would stay to haunt me later. Five years later, when my father passed away from cancer, I decided to continue the search for my sperm donor. I called the medical offices where I was created, and the receptionist seemed flabbergasted that I was searching for my bio dad. "I don't know what to say . . . I've never gotten a phone call like this!" she said, sounding stunned. I can't imagine how the clinic didn't receive these calls all the time now that AncestryDNA and 23AndMe were all the rage. Maybe this was just her go-to response to gaslight people who wanted answers about their true origins.

So, like any millennial, I spit in a tube and sent the specimen to AncestryDNA.com. Immediately after I registered my DNA, plenty of random second cousins, third cousins, and distant relatives emailed me trying to connect. I expressed no interest. The truth is, I had enough family members to try to keep track of already. I just wanted to see a photo of my biological father; that would be enough closure for me. "Did I look like him?" was my main question.

Time passed, and I paid little attention to the email alerts

AncestryDNA.com would send. I had other things I was interested in. Six years after spitting in that plastic tube, I got the message that I had been waiting for. A man claiming to be my long-lost biological brother sent me a direct message on my personal Facebook. "Hey Rachel! I know this is random, but I think you're my half-sister. I found your information on ancestrydna.com and it's a long story, but there are upwards of 25 of us DNA half-sibs! We all share the same bio-dad, aka sperm donor. If you want to know more, I messaged you on the site and gave you the genealogist's information to reach out to her if you would like. Best Wishes, Frank."

This seemed too peculiar to be real. How on earth was a person able to locate our sperm donor? Now that I had solid information, the quest felt less like a pipe dream. I immediately called the provided number and was able to get in touch with the genealogist. Once I spoke to her, she reassured me that she had already done all the necessary research on behalf of one of my half siblings. I had lucked out because my DNA data was on AncestryDNA.com, making it easy for her to contact me through Frank. She then directed me to my biological dad's real name and his Facebook profile photo, which I had been dying to see. I didn't have an urge to connect with him and I didn't want to reach out to him—I just wanted to see his fucking photo.

He looked like a less attractive version of my dad who had raised me, and I did see a slight resemblance to myself. He had wiry, unkempt eyebrows and thick brown hair, with an expression on his face that seemed aloof. His eye shape was similar to mine, a slight slant downward for that "bedroom eye" aesthetic that I so often get compliments on. All I could think about was what the doctor had told me: a couple of my half sibs had reached out to talk to him, but he wanted nothing to do with the situation. He was married with two children that he claimed as his and had never disclosed to his wife that he had nearly thirty other children running around.

Messages started flooding in, one after another, from people claiming to be my half siblings. I eventually learned that over twenty-five humans had been created with this donor's sperm that we knew about. What a strange realization to come to in my twenties! I thought the six siblings I grew up with were enough chaos to handle; I didn't need any more. But I hopped on the phone with Frank to get more information about this bizarre situation and understand how the other half sibs were feeling. Their reactions were all over the spectrum, some people more nonchalant than others. Some were absolutely furious. I felt rather removed from the news—it still seems surreal.

My group of half sibs decided to gather for a meet up in New York and asked me to join. I was on the fence about whether or not it was the right decision for me. I would be staying in a shared rental house with complete strangers and mingling all weekend long. At first, it seemed like a fun and interesting opportunity to connect with family. I committed to the event, because of course I wanted to unite with my siblings. But I watch too many crime documentaries and listen to too many podcasts to have actually gone through with it. I could have stayed at a neighboring home and then just visited them during the day, but the more I thought about it, the more I realized I didn't want to do it. The fear of being asked about my occupation repeatedly by newly discovered siblings was too much for me to fathom.

After I spoke with Frank, it sank in that they all knew what my profession was. They had inevitably googled me, which left me feeling grossed out and not interested in the whole "reunion." I cordially backed out and instead opted to read and look over the photos and information they so generously shared via email. Almost all of them had earned master's degrees, many of them were creatives, and all of them were at least 50 percent Jewish, like me. The curiosity about where I came from had been solved, and the yearning to see my biological father's face had been satisfied. I still dabble with getting to know the half sibs on a deeper level, and maybe someday I'll meet them in person, but for now, I'll keep it virtual. I facetimed one of my sisters recently.

The weight of my nearly thirty half sibs hangs heavy on me. It makes me think of sperm, embryos, donating—all the reproductive topics—in a new light. I used to think and feel like sperm donations were a good thing, and they are, but when you find out you have all these brothers and sisters that you never met, the concept seems outrageous. There should be a limit on how many times these men donate for money or ego. In the words of Elle Woods in *Legally Blonde*, "All masturbatory emissions where his sperm was clearly not seeking an egg could be termed reckless abandonment."

Sex Work

I toured a couple of colleges without feeling very drawn to their offered experiences. My mom and older sister had attended UCLA, one of the nation's premiere institutions. Growing up in Laguna Beach, the University of Southern California was the local dream school, but sadly, I didn't get in there, either. I was disappointed but not surprised, as I was aware my priorities had shifted. My father told me that I needed to stay home and go to a community college and then transfer to a four-year university. That would save him on rent, utilities, and living expense money that I would need if I were to attend a university away from home.

I had a very different idea of what I was doing, so I got a part-time job at Hooters because it looked fun and paralleled my vision of becoming a Playmate. Hooters offers plenty of modeling opportunities for their own brand. They also weigh you upon being hired, which seems illegal. And once you start working for them you can have one free meal each shift, so of course I gained weight. There is a training day where they teach you by video how to apply your makeup for the position. If you rip your nude stocking, then you must pay to replace it through a vending machine with your own money. It's expensive to be a Hooters girl. In contrast, the customers that come in are all shapes and sizes.

I really loved the outfits. I loved them so much, in fact, that I still own mine. In my super-short shorts and low-cut top, I was more than shocked when my father and my stepmom showed up to my place of business—mostly because I didn't tell either one that I was working there. My dad was fine with the choice. "It's a paying job!" he said with a sense of humor.

My stepmother, however, made her opinion known. "This is a disgusting place, I can't believe you're working here!" she said scathingly, right in the restaurant. She was never one to sugarcoat anything unless she was trying to manipulate someone.

I quit shortly after but told my dad that I would continue to work once getting up to Los Angeles to attend Santa Monica Community College; I just didn't tell him exactly what I was going to do for work. Sure, I had fucked up my grades in high school, but I knew I could do better. I managed to get nearly straight As while attending SMCC. I also met regularly with my school counselor to confirm that I was taking all the right classes and getting all the right credits to achieve that dream of a four-year institution. But was it even my dream? Or was it just something I felt pressured to do my whole life? I'm grateful for my education today, but I don't think a traditional degree is necessary for most people. Where I came from, it felt mandatory. In fact, there is an underlying message sent to young people that they must go to college, and if they don't then they are not legitimate, which is total nonsense.

I lived with two girls from Laguna, whom I'd attended high school, middle school, and elementary school with, but I was not very close to them. My father gave me enough money to live comfortably. However, I didn't have a credit card the way I did while living with my mom in high school. I had become accustomed to spending whatever I wanted. She used our father's child support, but she also put herself into credit card debt and had no limitations for us. This was the life I was used to. After she would take us on shopping sprees or let us use her credit card, she would complain incessantly about finances. "Ask your fathers for that child support check! They should be paying more than they pay. Why don't you ask them for money like you ask me for money, you spoiled brats!" she would scream. Money came from men and there was never enough to live the cushy way she wanted to live.

I was nineteen years old and desperately seeking an entry point into the *Playboy* world. I didn't quite know how to get noticed, but I wanted to be discovered. Craigslist back in the day was not as seedy as it is now. I searched for "*Playboy* modeling, *Playboy* jobs, *Playboy* gigs . . ." and an ad stood out to me. It was for a modeling job, specifically for *Playboy*. *Playboy*, after all, is a big brand with lots of products, and the scantily clad woman in the photo looked like a *Playboy* model to me—she was blonde and curvy and wore a boxing-themed outfit in a ring. I wasn't quite sure what the gig entailed, but I emailed the contact that was provided and expressed my interest. Within a day I got a phone call to meet up and interview for the position. I had a hunch that the role was not necessarily a modeling job by the time I met up with this madam in her white Benz in Beverly Hills.

"Do you have to have sex with the clients?" I recall asking.

"No, you don't always have sex," she told me—a total lie. I wonder if she thought I was undercover or didn't want to scare me off. Of course you have sex with the clients—this was an escorting job, not a modeling job at all! And thus, I became an escort.

Escorting carries a lot of stigma. It is the world's oldest profession—and possibly the world's most demonized profession. It's one that is more common than most people ever know, but one that so few can admit to engaging in because it's so vilified.

Prostitute is the word society likes to use for people who trade sex for money. Like many sex workers, I prefer *sex worker* because it doesn't sound like a slur. I also think many marriages are the long-term version of sex work. Trading money for sex is taboo if it's done with multiple men but very normalized if done with one, for life. This is my definition of the patriarchy.

The house where we worked was on Burton Way in Beverly Hills. The rate was low, like a thousand bucks a client or so, but I thought that it was fair at the time. I didn't know any better. I'd had sex in college for free and for fun with men I barely knew, so why was charging men I barely knew going to be any different? It didn't seem dangerous because of the location and the people running the operation seemed kosher, but I proceeded with caution. My first out-call (where you drive to another location, like a client's house or hotel room) was in Marina Del Rey. I was extremely nervous upon arriving at his condo and meeting this total stranger. I had braces on my teeth and a sort of innocence that made him and future clients nervous about my age—so nervous that I once had a lawyer client card me before we proceeded. This first client and I made out . . . for a while. That was gross in and of itself. Kissing is such an intimate act. I was so obviously scared of this man that he didn't even want to have intercourse with me. Instead, he asked for a blow job, and I agreed. As I went back into his room to perform the sex act, I was scared for my life. Not because of anything he had done, but because I was raised to be apprehensive of strange men and I didn't want to end up raped and killed in his back alley. This client was repulsive to me, but the money was decent, and after the encounter was over, the job seemed "easy." In retrospect, I conflated easy with "doable."

I didn't feel like I was doing something that was morally wrong, but I thought at the time it was technically illegal. It really depends on how you word the work, though. My client kept bringing up how I needed to make sure the agency blacked out my face in the photos because family members and friends could find my advertisements online. I was so clueless; I hadn't even thought of that. I liked the quick cash and the rebellious high that I got from doing the work. Men had always viewed me in a sexual way, and I thought, *Why not monetize that attention?* Also, Jeff, my high school sweetheart, had broken up with me for what I perceived as not fitting into his perfect image of a woman. So, for some reason, this felt like I was getting back at him. I *wasn't* getting back at him in real life, but it was some sort of retribution in my mind. I didn't think it was a step in the direction of modeling for *Playboy* once I realized what the job was, although I would soon learn that many *Playboy* models did escort work. And I felt desired doing the work, which I enjoyed.

While enrolled at SMCC, I registered for a class called The Sociology of Sex Work, taught by a tall, thin professor. She was a curious person, and to this day I still wonder why she taught that class. She was a sociologist who told us about how she experimented with eating pasta with her hands at a fancy steak house, just to see what the other diners' reactions would be. Was she at one point a sex worker herself? Did she want to be a sex worker? I honestly have no idea. I would love to go back in time and ask her. She had so many interesting conversations with us about sex work and the different tiers of the business. I was learning about this world while simultaneously escorting, stripping, and attending *Playboy* Mansion parties. I felt like I was a deep-diving journalist who was living and experiencing the topic that she was writing about.

I also felt like I knew more than everyone else in class—because I probably did. There was certainly truth to what the professor taught, although I feel like her idea of sex work was solely focused on money and social status. I don't recall her exploring the safety aspect of it. "Waitressing is a form of sex work!" was something she told us. "Escorts can get paid big money," she said, and that clocked. The academic arguments surrounding sex work would come later on at UCLA; this class was more neutral. The intellectual and social impact of sex work was absolutely fascinating to my eighteen-year-old brain. I'll never forget the lecture when she said, "Sex work is the only profession where your socioeconomic status doesn't match up with your paycheck." That stuck with me. I wonder what she would say today. Things really have changed since 2008.

I started taking strip aerobics at S Factor, a well-known class in LA. It felt freeing to be almost nude and moving my body as I chose, to the beat of the music. There were no mirrors, so I couldn't criticize myself like I could in a normal workout class. We got to wear eight-inch heels and learn choreographed dances in booty shorts. This expensive class soon transitioned into me becoming a dancer at a strip club. Once my writing professor walked into the club where I was dancing—or at least I think it was him. Working so close to school was risky, and I was always on edge as to whom I would run into. I asked my manager if I could skip the stage performance.

"You can just go home if you want to. That's awkward," he said. I just avoided the old guy in the dimmed room. Once, when I wasn't even working at the club, a girl I had befriended at school came in. She'd found out through a dancer that I worked there on occasion, and she wanted nothing to do with me because of it, immediately distancing herself. She brought it up one night and made sure I knew that she knew. I never heard from her again.

The job intimidates other women. The irony was that that classmate's mother was a *Playboy* Playmate. Those are the strange types of things that happened to me while studying and working as a sex worker at the same time. Even my dreams of becoming a *Playboy* Playmate needed to be hush-hush, because Hef didn't want strippers as his models or guests at his home. I felt so much shame from the outside world as a dancer. Listening to clients' issues and having to actually engage in conversation was not something I liked doing. I also was never one for anything illegal in the strip club, I was strictly dancing, so I never found the job to be lucrative. House dancing (where you are a dancer at a club regularly) just wasn't for me.

Women's Studies vs. the *Playboy* Mansion

For my junior year of college, I transferred from Santa Monica Community College to become a women's studies major at UCLA. My mom and my older sister had both gone to UCLA. I had wanted to go right out of high school, but I hadn't pulled the grades to get accepted. I had been distracted by filming the reality show; Jeff, the boyfriend I was obsessed with; and family drama. So I had to go to community college in order to transfer to the more prestigious school that I felt pressured to attend.

While at SMCC, I was moved by the women's studies classes I had randomly enrolled in. I couldn't believe I had gotten through eighteen years of life without learning about the ways in which race and gender shape American society. Had I ever heard of feminism? Sure. Had I ever heard of systemic racism? Yes. But I had no idea that white patriarchy was a fundamental and instrumental part of American capitalism. I was transfixed by these courses. Learning about domestic abuse, women's rights, and the social hierarchy of sex work lit my young mind up. I knew instantly that I was supposed to major in it.

During the week, I'd hear my fellow women's studies majors

attacking Hugh Hefner as a symbol of the patriarchy. On the weekends, I was part of the crowd of bikini-clad women vying for Hef's attention. I was a women's studies major gone wild.

How did I reconcile these two apparently conflicting worlds, my women's studies world of feminism at UCLA and my debauched *Playboy* Mansion world just up the hill? My reconciliation has to do with a concept I first learned in a women's studies class—and that impacts the life of every sex worker every day, including mine: the madonna-whore complex, also referred to as the virgin-whore dichotomy. It's a bit theoretical, but it explains my situation at that time perfectly—so buckle up for a little feminist theory.

The pattern was originally identified by Sigmund Freud, who noticed that many of his male patients were unable to respect a woman perceived by them as highly sexual—a perception that could be very broad. This inability leads many men to view their "marriage-material" wives as idealized, desexualized, "pure" women suitable for baby making (and unlikely to cheat). To gratify their sexual urges, they stray outside of marriage with promiscuous women whom they don't respect. Since the vast majority of older married men can't actually attract the hot young babes they lust after, they often turn to hiring sex workers, whom they judge most of all (yet still patronize to satisfy their sexual urges).

Feminists took the theory beyond the individual counseling room and applied it to wider cultural patterns within patriarchy. The essence of the madonna-whore dichotomy is a sharp division between "good girls" and "bad girls." The "good girls" are supposed to be chaste, sexually innocent, and pure, saving their virginity for their wedding night and never having a sexual thought for any other man besides their husbands. "Bad girls" are any women who dare express a wide-ranging sexuality outside of heterosexual, monogamous, child-producing marriages. Such women are considered "dirty," "sluts," and "whores" (even if they're not actually sex workers).

The virgin-whore dichotomy is one of the central features of patriarchal ideology, as it is one of the major cultural mechanisms by which men control women's sexuality. It started as a way for fathers to protect the "purity" of their daughters, so that their daughters could be married off to a "good" family in a union that would be economically advantageous to the parents. Once control of a young woman's fertility is passed over to her husband, the dichotomy further serves to guard her fertility from other men, ensuring paternal certainty (and avoiding cuckolding—that is, a man expending resources to raise another man's children).

I experienced versions of the madonna-whore dichotomy even before I became an escort, as a teen in Laguna Beach. When I became obsessed with watching *The Girls Next Door*, my high-status boyfriend could not have been more judgmental of the women on the show. He would say they were all sluts and whores and disgusting women.

One day while he was watching my favorite show with me, he went off on one of his rants about how disgusting the idea of women posing for *Playboy* was and how gross it looked. I announced, "Well, *I* want to be a *Playboy* Playmate one day!" He responded with "Why would you want that—it looks degrading." To me, it didn't look degrading, but rather, powerful. I watched Holly Madison direct a beautiful centerfold and create art. I watched documentaries on Stormy Daniels and Tera Patrick. I fangirled over Carmen Electra and Pamela Anderson. The Spice Girls were my first role models and Britney Spears my next. I loved women who were absolutely unashamed of their sexuality, regardless of what everyone else said about it.

My boyfriend had a traditional view of a woman's role in a relationship. "A woman shouldn't have a job outside of being a mother," he would say—a classic example of the madonna side of the dichotomy. He would also say, "My father told me to never marry a woman who's too attractive, because they'll cheat on you when you're on business trips."

I recall my boyfriend's friends telling him that I had been way too affectionate with them after I greeted them with kisses on the cheek. In all fairness, I had let his cousin finger bang me in the clubhouse pool a few years prior to meeting him, but that was eighth grade, and I was now a junior in high school. My reputation had preceded me. Perhaps that's why he tried to "own" me with a ring on my finger—that is, a promise ring that symbolized our future engagement and faithfulness to one another. I guess that didn't work out.

Though he didn't dump me on the spot when I told him I wanted to be a *Playboy* centerfold, I could see the commitment draining from his eyes in real time. He came from a conservative family. There was simply no way he could tell his parents, "Rachel is a *Playboy* Playmate this month!" I felt him distance himself from me after he realized that my interest in the show wasn't *just* about entertainment; my interest was also artistic and professional. He wanted a "good girl" as his girlfriend, not someone he perceived to be one of the "sluts" of *Playboy*. He slowly pushed me away and dumped me during my freshman year of college.

All of this slut-shaming is why the *Playboy* Mansion—when I did start going—felt so liberating and empowering to me. It was a place where my sexuality was welcomed, not shunned. It was a place where there was no shame in a woman being a highly sexual person. Sure, the rest of society might call us names, but we were just . . . *free.* Free to express our sexuality in a way that would *never* be accepted in polite society.

Of course, my women's studies colleagues wouldn't have viewed it as freedom. They didn't know that I was going up to the Mansion on weekends, but in women's studies circles, Hugh Hefner was viewed as the epicenter of the stereotypical "male gaze"—which he was. They would not have viewed my time at the Mansion as liberation, but rather as incarceration within narrowly defined gender roles.

However, for me, it did feel like freedom: freedom to pursue my dreams, and freedom from the judgments and slut-shaming of my social scene and my (now ex-) boyfriend. By being given free rein to celebrate and flaunt my sexuality, it felt as though I was busting out of the pure madonna role that my boyfriend had been expecting of me. My women's studies colleagues would have viewed it as stepping into another oppressive, male-defined gender role, that of the whore—who, according to the role, is valued not for her soul, spirit, or intellect, but solely for her body and her ability to gratify men sexually.

They had a point. If I had been an accomplished professor of quantum physics, without the looks or body I'd been blessed with by the genetic lottery, it's doubtful I'd have been invited back to the Mansion. Women were valued there for their looks, there's no doubt about it.

But in their critique of these sexualized gender roles and the male gaze, many of my women's studies professors and costudents engaged in their own form of the madonna-whore dichotomy, with a coat of feminist theory painted on. Good feminist women, according to them, would never be caught dead flaunting their bodies for the enjoyment of men, and if you did, you were a bad feminist. It felt like my boyfriend's judgmental attitude all over again.

It all led to a swirling inner conflict. I understood and agreed with the critiques of the male gaze from my classes. And yet I felt a strong desire to be validated in that gaze, and I felt clearly that was my choice; I didn't feel coerced by anyone specific into wanting what I wanted. I just wanted it, and I went for it. Not to mention, I was making a lot of money from that gaze, first as an escort and stripper and soon as a *Playboy* model and then a porn star.

Sex workers do not need to feel empowered by their work to deserve rights and respect, any more than waiters or factory workers do. That said, to me, my work in the adult industry has mostly felt empowering, because society tries to shame me for doing these things I want to do, but it's my choice and I do them anyway—and get paid for them. My body, my choice.

I'm not going to claim that the *Playboy* Mansion was some kind of feminist paradise—far from it. For me, however, it was a stepping-stone. A stepping-stone that allowed me to step past patriarchal sex-shaming and into greater sexual expression. But it was only the first step. I've attempted to integrate these different roles—the life of the mind and the life of the body—ever since then.

The thing I wanted most at the time was to be a Playmate. I was halfway there. I had a regular invite Friday through Sunday at Hugh Hefner's *Playboy* Mansion, which I had finagled while dancing at a gentlemen's club, Foreplay, in West LA. In order to work at Foreplay, I had to audition on stage on a Saturday night. I had to win a contest, which was judged by the guests' votes. I came in first place. This was quite the upgrade from the first strip club I had worked at, Silver Reign. Silver Reign had felt seedy, so I was ecstatic to be at this elevated location. I've truly always felt that a strip club is just for stripping. The man that invited and drove me up to Hef's mansion was like an undercover scout for Hef. He recruited young women from all over LA, and I just happened to be one of them.

I remember the day I met Hef like it was yesterday. I was wearing a skintight two-toned lavender-and-cream dress from American Apparel—that's what all the hott girls wore in 2008—

and a pair of sky-high, tan Guess heels. I did my hair and makeup like I was auditioning for a place in his world. I felt sexy but not quite as perfect as the other women, insecure about my adult braces and the bump on my nose. I had been drawn into the idea of Hef and all that he represented for years. This was my moment. I felt like my life was about to change, but I wasn't sure how.

We pulled up to the Mansion's big, ivy-covered gates, casually dropping that we were "On Hef's list for Fun in the Sun," something I had always wanted to hear. I gasped as we drove onto the property. The house was stunning. It looked like a castle surrounded by a lush green lawn, shady trees, and beautiful landscaping. Pretty, colorful peacocks wandered the grounds, like something out of a fairy tale. My heart fluttered and my anxiety kicked up a notch. Was I really going to meet Hugh M. Hefner? It felt surreal.

We found Hef holding court at the end of his long wood dining room table, surrounded by many people I recognized from the show *The Girls Next Door*. Exotic monkeys, modeling careers, a built-in sorority, and a mansion—what was there not to love? Hef and I were introduced, and the moment our hands touched, I knew the *Playboy* Mansion was where I belonged. The rest of the evening was a blur, but I left with the distinct feeling that I could be whatever I wanted to be. Transitioning from being a super fan of the *Girls Next Door* television show to a selected guest of Hef's at the *Playboy* Mansion felt like a fantasy. My dream was happening before my very eyes, and nothing could stop me from becoming a Playmate.

A few days later, one of Hef's assistants, Jenny, invited me back for Friday and Saturday Movie Night and a Saturday and Sunday party called Fun in the Sun. I had been hand-selected by Hef. *What an honor!* I thought to myself. By the time I transferred from SMCC to UCLA, I was at Hef's every weekend, Fridays,

Saturdays, and Sundays. I dedicated all my extracurricular time to the Mansion and the girlfriends I had met there. It made it really challenging to join a sorority or involve myself on campus at UCLA, because I already had a community and a party house taking up my time—it just happened to be the *Playboy* Mansion.

I made friends with the other regular guests, models, and testing Playmates at the house. I loved the carefree environment and my world there. As time passed, I realized I wanted more than anything to become a Playmate. They had all the attention and recognition that I so wished for. Having gotten my boobs and nose done by Hef's favorite surgeons—with a discounted fee for being a model—I was ready for my title as a beauty. But I also knew from spending time at the Mansion with Playmates who were testing and staying at the Bunny House that it was a competitive and cutthroat process. Furthermore, becoming a staple in Hef's home had muddied the waters. He had certain places for the people in his life. One unspoken rule was that if I was a part of his regular lineup socially, then he really didn't want to grant me the position of Playmate, because what would stop me from bailing on Saturdays and Sundays? There were so many other women he had made Playmate who had just up and left afterward. He still did it on occasion, but it was rare, and I took note. I also had it in my head that he might want to see someone new and fresh in his glossy pages, not necessarily a woman he saw every week. I worried I was aging out already at the ripe age of twenty-one. My worst fear was "If he was going to make me a Playmate, then he would already have done it . . ." The insecurities and self-doubt were endless. It tore me up inside. Was I not pretty enough?

As more time passed, I realized I also wanted to be one of Hef's girlfriends. He had anywhere from two to ten girlfriends at a time. Basically, this meant living at the Mansion, being Hef's arm candy, and looking pretty at various *Playboy* parties and events, plus having sex with him once a week and having most of your living expenses paid for, including an allowance. It was basically being Hef's sugar baby—which was fine by me. It seemed glamorous, and it was exactly what I wanted.

I saw no reason why I couldn't join their ranks. But I also knew damn well from watching *The Girls Next Door* that getting into his inner circle was motivated and rivalrous. His existing girlfriends weren't exactly welcoming; they played defense against any would-be girlfriend attempting to join their ranks.

I wrote Hef a letter, explaining how I felt about him: "Dear Hef, I've sincerely loved staying at your house during the weekends. Friday, Saturday, and Sunday night movie night are so much fun and I am learning so much about classic film. I am enrolled now at UCLA and I love that it's so close to your house. Crystal [his main girlfriend at the time] seems nice and I'm happy I'm getting to know her. [Lie.] Just wanted to let you know how much I love the *Playboy* mansion and the *Playboy* family. I hope to see you more." I continued trying to get his attention by writing him thoughtful letters like this and placing them in the gold envelope holder, shaped like a vagina, at the top of his stairs.

Hef picked who got painted as the decadent "painted girl" at big parties—a coveted role. I was selected for this honor for his annual, legendary Midsummer's Night Dream party. A-list Hollywood celebrities were regulars at these parties, including Leonardo DiCaprio and Owen Wilson. But for me, I was just excited to be painted. I had seen Kendra Wilkinson do it on *The Girls Next Door*, and I had always dreamed of doing it, even though it meant hours of labor—standing, drying, being repainted, airbrushed, drying, perfected, photographed, and then prancing around the party as decor.

I was a hit at the party. I don't think anyone else had so many people come up to them asking for photos. But on another level,

I felt deeply insecure. The most beautiful and vaunted women in the *Playboy* universe, including the esteemed centerfolds, come to these parties, plus all the Hollywood celebrities. I put them all on pedestals. Becoming a centerfold was the only thing that mattered to me at that time in my life.

Even though I was a star that night because of my beautiful body paint "outfit," my low self-esteem was wearing on me. There must be few places on the planet where women second-guess themselves about their looks more than the Mansion—which is ironic, because the whole premise is that those hanging out there are among the most beautiful women in the world. But we were all competing for attention and favors from one very overextended man, who was so used to good-looking women that we could easily pass through these events unnoticed by him. I couldn't even get up the nerve to approach Hef in his cabana, with his bevy of beauties—in part for fear of provoking the judgment of the women guarding their territory from new interlopers.

The notes were just the beginning of my attempt to woo Hef. He loved thoughtful gifts and especially photos, so I arranged a photo-shoot of my new breasts and nose with my dear late friend Eddie Wolf. Eddie had photographed Beyoncé, Whitney Houston, and so many more legends. I couldn't believe he wanted to shoot me!

I curated a down-to-earth country girl ensemble, though with glam makeup. I also remembered to bring a cigar and boating cap—Hef's signature look. I met Eddie on a yacht at a marina. His gorgeous photos gave me hope that I would be the next Play-mate. I carefully selected the sexiest and cutest ones for Hef. He loved cute, young, and angelic, and I was that

Crystal must have found my letter with the photos. I gave Hef my cute photos by Eddie Wolfe myself. One night at dinner, she said, "I really wish you girls would stop writing Hef letters. It's really rude and unnecessary to do that. He reads them before bed." That same night she had friends visiting from out of town, and in a passive-aggressive tone, introduced me as "Rachel, the girl I was telling you all about." Maybe she didn't like that Hef framed one of the photos I gave him and placed it in his room.

She clearly saw me as up-and-coming competition. (And I don't blame her, because that's exactly what I was trying to be.) She always gave me dirty looks. She was as ice-cold as the frozen yogurt in the yogurt runs, which she never invited me to after movie nights with the other girls.

Years later, one of Hef's ex-girlfriends, Amanda, friended me on Instagram. She lived at the Mansion at the same time I was a regular and was always very distant and cold toward me. I always wanted to befriend her and Crystal, but with their dirty looks and one-sentence responses, they made it clear they didn't want to engage. His girlfriends and I were always in the same room during movie nights, but the social hierarchy was clear. I was not fucking Hef, and I was not his official live-in girlfriend. I was a threat to Crystal and her power, along with the other Fun in the Sun girls. Any one of us could come in and take her spot as number one, and she knew it. Amanda and I bonded through Instagram about home decor, family life, and babies. I asked her, "Was there something that I did that upset Crystal or made her treat me the way she did when we were both up there?" I always felt like she either ignored me or sneered at me, and I didn't deserve that.

She quickly responded, "Yes, she was incredibly insecure about people trying to swoop in on her position, so she just assumed everyone was a threat. I remember she told Hef that you worked in adult films. A couple days later, he had someone from the office put some of your content on a DVD for him to watch, and she was so upset! It's funny looking back at how petty people could be. Toward the end of his life, she hardly let anyone come visit the mansion. Hef would ask Allison and Joel [his besties] where all the girls were, and they didn't have the heart to tell him that his wife stopped that tradition. People weren't even allowed to call him. She would intervene on that too! Same with all the letters and cards that women sent to him. She would read them and they would go into the trash. A lot of times she would take girls off the invite list based on letters."

I was shocked. All this time I never knew what really happened, and I never had the communication that I needed. I thought Hef had decided to kick me out on his own. I honestly felt like I had imagined his numerous letters to my little studio apartment in Westwood. Like it was all a dream. I had so many questions about why I was kicked out so abruptly, and if I was as relevant to him as I felt I was at the time. This little bit of explanation gave me closure.

Nevertheless, even with all of this going on, I decided to give *Playboy* stardom one more shot. All I wanted in life was to be a Playmate. Hanging around all the other Playmates, I constantly asked myself, "Am I not Playmate-worthy? Am I not beautiful? Why has Hef not already plucked me from his bevy of beauties to ask me to pose for the centerfold?" Hugh Hefner's acceptance of me meant the absolute world to me—and to every woman around him.

But why? It was as if his view of me represented the view that all men had of me. Few men in the world have had as many world-class knockouts vying for his attention and approval—which meant, if he gave it to you, you *must* be gorgeous. It felt like power. And I wanted to get near the top of this power hierarchy. I decided I needed to do something about it.

I had already posed for many of *Playboy*'s special-edition magazines, including "Fresh New Faces" and "Sexy Summer

Girls," and I was even named *Playboy*'s UCLA Girl of the Pac-10 in *Playboy* magazine. Many models go on from these special editions to become Playmates and even Playmate of the Year! *So I'm a shoo-in, right?* I reassured myself.

At this point I had spent a couple of years of my life coming up every Friday, Saturday, and Sunday. I was dedicated. I had taken a million photos with Hef. I had bantered and flirted with him constantly, he had kissed me on the cheek a hundred times, and I had idolized the Playmates around the house. It was my turn to shine! I decided that there was only one way to make my dreams come true, and that was to ask directly for what I wanted. So I wrote Hef another letter.

"Dear Hef, I have enjoyed every minute of my experience up here at the Mansion and I love spending my weekends with the girls. I love modeling and it would be my dream and absolute honor to be considered for Playmate. I was wondering if I could test for Playmate?" And that was all it took. He said yes to a photo test (a tryout before the real shoot).

The photographer was Arny Freytag, the most famous and respected centerfold photographer at the time. I had followed him and his career for years, and now *I* was going to shoot my test with *him*! Iconic. I felt like everything I had been doing was in preparation for this moment in my life. I couldn't have been more excited. It felt surreal walking into the studios in my comfy sweats and hopping into hair and makeup. The wardrobe girl pulled some lingerie for me, and Arny snapped back at her, "Change this set—my models wear Agent Provocateur." My backdrop was a light-pink, feminine set, with little white faux windows and a white couch.

The entire setup was very innocent, with teen girl vibes. This is still a vibe I relate to. I'm a girly girl at heart, and this aesthetic really did express my personality. I was normally comfortable being nude and in lingerie, but at this moment, I was nervous. Nervous about whether I was going to model correctly, nervous about how good the photos were going to be, and nervous to see if Hef would approve.

Shooting with Arny was heaven. I'd never been so happy in all my life. Arny was professional, artistic, and patient. He was used to working with brand-new models who don't know how to pose for a camera. "You're a natural," he said to me as he snapped his camera. I would come to learn that not all photographers make it so easy. He would tell me to adjust my pose or posture slightly— "Turn here, arch there"—but in a way that was receptive and kind. (Which, I've since learned, is all too rare.) To him it was probably just another day at work; to me it was going to change my life. I felt like I was finally being seen. I had made an impression on Hef, and I was finally getting my *Playboy* test!

Hef brought the shoot up to me in person afterward at movie night. I tried to express my gratitude by telling him how much I enjoyed it. "I could do that every day," I said passionately. It was nerve-racking talking to Hef. I always stuttered or couldn't articulate what I wanted to say because so much was on the line, which is completely unlike me. I should have said, "Thank you so much for making my dream come true," but the words slipped from my mouth. It was so much easier to pen letters to him than to get out what I wanted to say in real life.

Unfortunately, a few weeks later I got a call from *Playboy* Studios. I hadn't made the cut. I wasn't going to be a centerfold, and I wasn't even going to be one of the other models with a full set in the magazine. All they could do for me was publish my photos online. I was *Playboy*'s Cybergirl of the Month, they informed me, their enthusiasm lost on me as the news of my failure sank in.

I knew Hef made this decision; he made *all* the decisions about who was going to become a centerfold. I never got up the courage to ask him why I didn't make the cut; I regret I never did.

The relationship between Hef's role as editor and his desire to have lots of gorgeous women around (who were mostly there vying to get the modeling opportunities he could dole out to them) was complicated. Looking back, this dynamic has a decidedly pre–#MeToo feel.

Hugh Hefner died just a week before the *New York Times* published its exposé of Harvey Weinstein, sparking mass awareness of and participation in the #MeToo movement, which Tarana Burke had started in 2006. While Hef's relation to women was not (as far as I know) criminal like Weinstein's, there was definitely a predatory casting-couch vibe to the whole scene. I never slept with Hef, but many ladies surmised that doing so upped one's chances of becoming a girlfriend or getting *Playboy* modeling opportunities, and so they threw themselves at him. I didn't see that working out often; I regularly saw him quickly lose interest after getting what he wanted. But he was always dangling that *possibility* of opportunity.

The complication was, there was a limit to how many new modeling opportunities Hef could offer—but there was no limit to how many modelworthy young women he wanted to fuck. He never asked for or proposed sex with the young new aspirants; that wasn't his style. Nonetheless, a lot of women came to the conclusion—not unfounded—that asking *him* to have sex might mean they get more of his attention and have a higher chance of becoming a girlfriend.

That said, there were plenty of girls who went to his bedroom after a party and didn't get anything more out of it than sex with a distracted, Viagra-enhanced elderly man. And in those cases, Hef hadn't reneged on any promises, because he never made any.

He had just worked out a lifestyle in which gorgeous women constantly flung themselves at him, hoping for a shot at stardom.

What Hef wanted even more than sex was having tons of arm candy hanging around; the only thing he wanted stroked more than his cock was his ego. To maximize the number of beautiful women around him, he worked out a delicate balance of stringing women along with smaller gigs like Cybergirl of the Month, dangling the potential for future opportunities. That potential—unlikely ever to get fulfilled—kept plenty of pretty women hanging around. Including me.

There was always an underlying tension among the women on the weekends. What did each one want? Would any of us ever get Playmate? Did Hef want us as girlfriends? Is the new girl staying at the Bunny House pretty enough to be a Playmate? Who did Hef have sex with? What's going to happen to her now? Who's going to be selected as a painted girl? Will I get invited to the New Year's party? So many questions filled our minds those years at Hef's.

Hef kept aloof from all this, which was the perfect way of keeping us in the dark. He knew that the more we competed with each other for his attention . . . well, the more attention he got! And he loved it, even though it often felt awful to most of us.

I have complicated feelings about all of this. I feel grateful for the fun times I had at the Mansion, and the modeling opportunities I did receive through it—I couldn't have imagined a more fun way to spend my college years. But looking back, I think it's fair to say the power dynamics and manipulation Hef put in play at *Playboy* would not have survived the #MeToo era, which exploded internationally just a week after Hef died.

Being rejected by Hef, I felt like a loser. But before I let the disappointment spin out, I remembered my idol, Jenna. Her image gave me strength. *Fuck it*, I thought to myself. *I'm not going to wait around so Hef can tell me that I'm good enough to be a fucking centerfold in* Playboy. *I'm going to be like Jenna Jameson. I'm going to do porn, and I'm going to make movies, and I'm going to be a Penthouse Pet. And I don't give a fuck.*

That anger I felt created a boiling point in which I found the drive I'd always needed to get into porn. I was ready.

A Pornographic
Reflection

*Writing is like sex. First you do it for love, then you do it for
your friends, and then you do it for money.*

— VIRGINIA WOOLF

I had been escorting and modeling for a year or so by now.
I googled. I researched. I emailed. I found Jim South World
Modeling, Jenna Jameson's old agent, in the San Fernando Valley.
He was nice enough, but I didn't feel like his run-down, rinky-
dink office and the companies he wanted to book me with were
on my level of professionalism. I am inherently an elitist—always
have been. Coming from Laguna Beach, it's in my blood. Shortly
after this meeting, I unknowingly signed a five-year contract with
an "agent" named John, who owned a company called Matrix
Models. I wanted desperately to get out of this contract, as he
didn't book me any work over the period of a couple months I was
signed to him. I was confused because I thought I could at least
get a basic job in porn. Mainstream film had made it look so easy.

I had signed my youth away to some random guy who promised me he would put me in magazines and in movies. Not to
exonerate myself, but college hadn't prepared me for this one. My

experience was stereotypical—I felt like I was in a bad film about a porn star. I had given my modeling rights over to an old, white man, which would soon become a recurring theme in my life. He had trapped me in an agreement that I couldn't shoot content at all without him booking me the job or without me giving him a percentage of my income. *How fucking stupid was I to have done this*, I thought as he phoned me while I was visiting my unofficial boyfriend in New York. He called to tell me that he would take me to court if I dared to shoot without his permission. He must have found out I was submitting myself to other agencies.

It is important to mention that after my father's death I needed to get a job to support myself. Otherwise, I would have to be under the supervision and control of my stepmother, Darcy. She had rules for me if I was going to continue to live off the money she had stolen from my father. I say "stolen" because she had my father signing paperwork and changing his will while he was heavily medicated. This was not something proven in a court of law, but I certainly witnessed it. She demanded that I stay in school full-time if she was going to continue to support me financially. I was only enrolled at UCLA as a part-time student, and I hadn't budgeted for this living/school expense—my father had always taken care of it. Being a full-time student would immensely limit my ability to get into the adult film industry, where I could build a brand and make money instantly and independently without relying on anyone. I would also be on a stricter budget now that my dad was gone and Darcy was giving all his money to her children.

I went back to the old millennial drawing board, Google. I searched for the most popular adult film stars. Tori Black and Alexis Texas popped up first. Recently, while I was staying in a hotel room with a girlfriend, I had watched a movie starring Tori. I had never seen anyone have sex with such passion and intensity.

She was not only talented but voracious. Women in mainstream films are not featured in the same way they are in adult films. No, I don't mean seeing "the pink," which means women's genitals. I don't mean the wild sex, either; I mean that the women in these videos seemed powerful. I loved watching the confidence that they seemed to have. I thought, *Who else shows this amount of fearlessness in their work?* I had always strived to have such confidence, but the way they seemed to feel about their bodies was not represented in film outside of porn or in real life. The popular performers seemed to come from one agency, LA Direct Models. I decided I would submit my photos to them and hope for the best; maybe an agent would see me and think, *That's the next Jenna.* I got an immediate response: Victoria, LA Direct's assistant, requested that I come in person to meet the owner and lead agent, Devon Roy. Remember that name for later.

I walked into to the office building housing Vivid, the company that Kim Kardashian and Paris Hilton had signed their sex tapes over to, located in Studio City, California, on Ventura Boulevard. I was headed to the number-one adult agency at the time, known for creating adult superstars. I had snapped a photo of the iconic signage outside in hopes to upload the image to my Facebook page—partially to get attention, partially to update all my friends about my next phase in life. I felt giddy and nervous and so fucking excited about becoming a porn star. I wish I was still that ecstatic about work. I was intrigued by the idea of it, and that it was tangible. I walked into Devon's open, spacious white office, hoping he'd approve of my look and ambition. Approval from other people has always been a subject I've struggled with, while at the same time I've made controversial choices that most people are bound to disapprove of. A strange inner conflict to repeatedly endure.

Devon was the owner and agent there, and I knew that he made the big-named girls, well, big. I was twenty-one years old, tan, blonde, and eager . . . what was not to love as a porn agent? My angst and self-doubt came when I realized that my hometown friends and family would see my legs spread open. I had this realization: *Oh my god, they are going to see these photos, and what are they going to think?* Explicit porn has a different connotation then softcore *Playboy*-style porn, doesn't it? *Why?* I kept asking myself.

I asked Devon, "Is this safe?" He wasn't completely dishonest. He explained that a case of sexual assault had taken place on set that week, specifically in a shower. The male talent had raped the female performer after the scene. She didn't want to press charges, probably because she was fearful of being laughed at by law enforcement or openly slut-shamed. I was shocked, but the story didn't turn me away from the career. *That wouldn't happen to me*, I thought.

I was also fearful of the potential for pain. How on earth would something the size of a performer's penis ever fit inside me? I asked Devon, "Does it hurt?" He said usually it did not, but sometimes it could, depending on the situation and the film. This one would have been a difficult question to really answer unless he was a woman . . . so I can give him a break here. Kind of. The truth is, yes, sometimes on-set sex hurts because it's vigorous and long. Filming a scene takes time and patience. There are cuts in production—they need more angles, more footage, more time, just more. Bodies are not really built for this type of physical labor, but that is why performers get paid well, and it just comes along with the job. I was nervous about this aspect. I've never liked pain. With no one to really turn to, I felt alone.

Although I knew this decision would cause controversy on the home front (no idea just how much, though), it was a lot easier to make now that my father was deceased. When he was alive, my dad was not thrilled that I was modeling nude. He thought it was neat I was hanging out at the *Playboy* Mansion, but I recall him asking me from his bed, while he was sick with cancer, "What did I do wrong to make you want to do such a thing?" I don't see the correlation to this day, but I did assure him that he didn't do anything wrong, even if he might have. Maybe he gave me a little too much power to do whatever I wanted to do? Maybe the topless paintings of women around the house were too much of an influence? Maybe I was a born exhibitionist? Maybe because he was divorced from my mom and wasn't around as much as he could have been, I felt more free to explore this career path? Maybe something darker. . . . All this was going through my mind, but it wasn't enough to turn me away from changing my life trajectory forever.

Devon was intimidating, with piercing blue eyes and a thick English accent. He reminded me of what Lucifer might look like. He wore a light-blue button-down business shirt and a pair of well-fitted khaki pants. His handshake was firm and his eye contact intense. His eye color looked almost fake because of how illuminated his irises were. He was in superb physical shape as well, still performing on occasion under the stage name Ben English. He had a highly self-assured air about him. It's a very intoxicating quality. Devon was charming, and his strength and confidence made me feel safe. I was immediately intrigued and attracted to him. He had me fill out a checklist that listed each explicit sex act, such as anal, BDSM, boy-boy-girl (that sounded fun), and so on. I was then instructed to check each one I was comfortable doing off the list. I wasn't comfortable with much. I was coming into the business very closed-minded when it came to my own sexuality and taboo sex acts. I just hadn't experimented much past vanilla, heterosexual sex.

Devon was instantly a very stable presence in my life. All the models he represented called him "Daddy D." He would bail them out of jail, make sure they had work when he wanted them to—and sometimes when they didn't want to. I had no idea what lies he had hidden at the time, or that in 2019 he would be under investigation for allegations of sex trafficking.

I was asked to go into a room in his clean, white office space. He followed me in and closed the door. He stood four feet away from me, examining me from head to toe in a very clinical way. It didn't feel creepy. He seemed professional at the time. The room was plain, with a conference table and fax machine. He asked me to undress to make sure that the photos that I had submitted were accurate. Photo editing had become all the rage, and models' portfolios often didn't match up with their actual aesthetic in person. I felt anxious for his approval. I really wanted to sign with a top agency that would book me modeling and acting work. There is this misconception that getting consistent work in the adult industry as a woman is easy or basic; for me, it was not. In today's world anyone can Photoshop themselves into whatever it is they dream up. Women can erase bad tattoos; they can make themselves taller, prettier, and younger. Then when they show up in person for go-sees (auditions), they are often turned away.

I took off my clothes, something I was comfortable doing, and I turned around, exposing myself so that he could see everything, including my fully shaven vulva. "Well . . . Rachel, I think you're going to work a lot," he said matter-of-factly. And just like that, he walked out of the room.

We mapped out what sex acts I was going to be performing for my career timeline. We decided that I was going to start with just solo video work, then girl-on-girl action (which I had never really done before), and boy-girl work. That was what I was most excited for. That is what they call it when someone has hetero-sexual sex on film. My UCLA professor told me that the term was infantilizing, but since both genders were being called youthful nouns, I wasn't offended. He now had my checklist to confirm I was comfortable with all the sex acts I would be booked to do. I didn't have a preference list of men, because I hadn't met any male performers other than Devon himself. He had a "no list" of his very own for me, though. Some of the guys on his no-list for me were sexy, too—major bummer.

But first we had to get rid of John, the incompetent agent from Matrix Models. I told Devon about how I was signed with him, and he listened intently, eyes steady. Devon could make you feel like he truly cared about you just by the way he gave his full attention. He seemed to be thinking of a solution. He said, "Rachel, we will pay him off." When Devon said *we*, he meant *me*, and by payment, he offered John a couple thousand dollars, which at the time seemed like a lot of money. I wanted to sign with LA Direct Models, so I agreed to it. Devon told me that the payment would buy me out of my five-year contract, but it felt like John was abusing his powers; after all, he had never booked me a single job.

Before getting my booking info as a model, I received a phone call. In the beginning, I remember being enthusiastic when getting phone calls because they meant work; later on, I would be annoyed by the phone calls because they would mean work. These feelings fluctuated from time to time.

Devon came from a musical background. He had gone on tour with the Rolling Stones, Aretha Franklin, and other big-name musicians to help coordinate shows and do stage management. He referenced these tours often, and I believe that his experience in the music business is what made him unique as a porn agent. He seemed to have a long-term plan in mind for his models, even if that came at a cost. If I told Devon I had special days I wanted to be off work, those were respected. Now, if I hadn't stated I was off those dates, he would book me for the acts I had checked on my yes list. I couldn't get out of the bookings once he had his mind set on a job. I would need to pay a break fee, which was some made-up amount that would compensate him for his loss of profit, and herein lay the problems that would catch up to him later: sex work isn't like any other work; you can't legally be forced to perform. He had a way of making models feel as if they had a legal obligation to do so. They didn't.

How much do porn stars get paid? Rates are a sensitive subject, because they vary based on your profitability in the marketplace. Distinguishing the difference between my self-worth as a human and my worth as an entertainer can be tricky. My agent suggested a rate, and I agreed to it. I would set my rate higher based on the number of years I had been performing and different sex acts I was comfortable doing. Then I would get an email from the agency listing all the important details of the shoot I had been booked for, whether that was a script or a call time and location—all the important info should have been in the email. Sometimes major details, like the location of the production or even what site it was for, were left out. When I was a new performer, I was booked almost every day for two months or so. My demand decreased over time, but I would still get consistent work. Then there was the fear that work would dry up completely; this is referred to as "being shot out." No one wants to be shot out. The implication is that fans are over seeing you because you have shot so many scenes. As a performer I had little control over whether fans wanted to watch me or companies wanted to book me, which was frustrating.

The next step in becoming an adult film actress was a photo shoot for LA Direct Models, kind of like head shots for mainstream actors, but these also involved my nude body. On this particular day, I remember my makeup artist doing a good job on my face but having a horrible attitude. When I asked the other models what the boy-girl sex scenes were like, she had the audacity to say, "It's not like they make love to you, Tasha!" Her tone of voice was rude and her energy was bad, something I would learn affects the whole set. Once I took these still modeling shots for advertisement on the website, I then went on go-sees, where I would meet directors in person at their studios. This was not compensated, and a driver or agent would accompany me. Then it was time to get tested.

STD testing is scary because needles are horrible. I have always been petrified of being poked with a needle. How could someone who is so terrified by needles end up in a job that requires mandatory blood and urine testing every two weeks? That's a question I would often ask myself as I lay down in the testing facility for fear of passing out. The mainstream adult community tested at just two facilities in Los Angeles. Supposedly, these doctors are more in touch with the industry and the technology is more advanced for detecting HIV. It is a self-governed system, which makes it controversial and not as efficient as it would be if there were more oversight from a protected union or by some special interest group that had our best interest in mind. Neither the FSC (Free Speech Coalition) nor APAC (the Adult Performer Advocacy Committee) does an adequate job in protecting adult performers. I would know; I served as the chairperson of the APAC and got see up close how the system operates—and the lack of safety and security adult performers have.

Having sex is always risky, but when you get tested for most STDs, including the dreaded human immunodeficiency virus, before engaging in it, it's less risky. Using the PASS (Performer Availability Screening Services) system, we have been able to prevent HIV from spreading on adult film sets for over a decade. That is something that made me feel safe, even though it was not a guaranteed result—nothing in sex is guaranteed. I guess you could say that I feel more confident having sex with a performer because their livelihood depends on if they are negative or not.

In entertainment many performers use stage names, from music to acting, but in the adult business, it's even more common. There is a myriad of reasons why people choose to do this. Before the days of the internet, it was easier to disguise what you did for work with a stage name. Furthermore, for safety reasons, many performers want to hide their identity from stalkers, fans, or even family, so changing their name is a step in doing so. It is my belief that in 2023 there is no point in trying to hide one's identity. It is a pillar that I live by, "live in the light," so I am open and honest with just about everyone when it comes to what I do. That being said, I would still probably choose a stage name if I were getting into adult today, because it is nice to have separation from a character I play in videos and photos for other people's enjoyment.

When coming up with my stage name, I asked my mom what names she liked. I brought up "Tasha," and we both thought it seemed fitting. When it came to my last name, Silver Reign was the name of the first strip club I ever danced at, so "Reign" was both nostalgic and means domain or rule over something. Devon asked me what my stage name would be and told me that I should choose one. I chose Tasha Reign. I don't like when fans refer to me as Rachel just because they know that is my real name. They don't know me outside of Tasha, and it implies that they do. I also don't love when people outside of entertainment purposes call me Tasha, like they only see me as a porn star. Now, because of the internet, I will take my future husband's last name in order to have an identity outside of porn, something I wasn't originally planning on doing, but feel like I have to now. I like the separation of church and state.

In most adult film production, there are a series of steps that are taken before a video is made. If you're on an aboveboard, mainstream adult film set, you will need to prove your age. You will need to fill out tons of paperwork, and sometimes you will have to film an exit video explaining that you are not being trafficked or held against your will, essentially stating that you consent to everything that went on during production. That's when ethics get questionable. I don't think we should have to make those videos. They feel like blackmail, a way that a shady director could somehow "prove" consent took place, even if it didn't. "Are you here of your own free will?" and "Can you confirm you're doing a boy-girl scene today?" are common prescene questions that a director may ask you before filming. Imagine for one second that you're a woman who just got assaulted by the man who is asking you exit video questions: "Did the shoot go as planned?" Or my favorite: "Were you treated fairly?" and you can't get your paycheck for the work you just performed unless you say yes. What in the actual fuckery? The paperwork discloses that the production house can use the content in any way they see fit, forever. Once you do something on film, it is out for everyone to see, because of the internet. Many times I would shoot for one person and it would be sold to someone else or end up on another website. Producers monetize the content in the most efficient way possible without consulting the talent. As I type this, I wish the age to perform legally was twenty-one. It's such a huge decision to make at eighteen—the human brain doesn't finish developing until age twenty-five.

The Good
"Rolling, and action!" I was clitoris to mouth on my first ever girl-girl adult movie set, for *Penthouse*. I couldn't have been happier—or more nervous. I was excited that my dream of becoming the next Jenna Jameson could possibly come true. I also knew that *Penthouse* magazine had centerfolds, so I hoped that day on set I

could catch the attention of the editor, Kelly Holland, who might think I was centerfoldworthy. I loved the glossy pages of men's magazines, the celebrated foldout poster of the woman of the month looking so dreamy. I was always bisexual, so for me this idea was not only an aspiration but a turn-on. I loved the idea of being every fan's favorite model to gaze at when they were having their private time alone. I always thought that would be so intimate. I had been working out, doing yoga every day to make sure I felt my best in front of the camera.

The amount of work I was putting into my looks was insane. Hair, skin, body: it is a full-time job—an expensive full-time job. Ash Hollywood was my castmate. She was the hot new starlet with a flat chest, long blonde hair, and masculine energy. First, we got into hair and makeup and the artists transformed us from regular "girl-next-door" types to stunning vixens with pink and blue streaks in our hair. We wore heavy eye makeup and light-pink lip gloss on our plump, pouty lips. I was anxious because I had never had sex on film before, I had never had sex with a woman, and I didn't even know if I would be good at it. I was fucking nervous and extremely self-aware. In modeling you need to be hyperaware of your figure, but in acting you need to completely let go and not be self-conscious. In porn, you must do both. Today when people ask me what my job is, it's difficult to choose model or actress because of this. Ash seemed to have everything under control; she clearly knew what she was doing and made me feel more at ease. She was so loud, so pretty, and so good at what she did. She was a fantastic performer.

After an hour or two of makeup and hair, I looked gorgeous, and Ash and I were put into wardrobe to finish up the looks. We had two different sets that day—a set is a look and a theme for photos and usually a matching video. The theme was a Rachel Zoe television show parody, and I was giddy. I didn't even know how to have sex with a woman, but luckily for me, Ash had enough experience that she just took over. She was soft, pretty, and smelled great. As you have sex with more and more people, especially strangers, you realize how pivotal a role olfactory senses play in intercourse.

Ash used her tongue and fingers. She checked in with me about what I liked and didn't like. That thorough form of consent between people was introduced to me on porn sets. As young adults, we aren't always taught to negotiate what acts are going to happen, but in porn it's a must. I owe a lot to porn; my knowledge of the human body is one of those subjects that I truly thank the adult industry for educating me about. I remember being asked to pose for photo stills, called "pretty girls" in the industry, which were taken before the scene, which is a routine I got used to. There is a lot of specific lingo that the industry uses, like calling outsiders "civilians." My scene with Ash is a blur, both because it was so long ago and because I was so nervous. Ash ended up being a friend of mine and someone I worked on movies with throughout my career. I admired her physicality and flexibility, her strength and her beauty. I couldn't help but think, *Wow, now this is art.*

I imagined myself working like this regularly and thought how easy and freeing a job like this could be compared to escort work. I would still finish my college education, but on my own schedule, not under Darcy's rules. I hoped that my photos and videos would be released soon and that I could post them on social media. I wasn't thinking of a boyfriend or a future husband or dating at all. I was twenty-one years old and thinking about life in the present and about the Louis Vuitton bags I wanted to buy. I was eager to see what was going to come next. I was also scared that I would drift even further away from my Laguna friends than I already had.

I keenly remember leaving work that day excited about what the next chapter in my career would bring me, proud that I was working for *Penthouse* and wildly independent with the knowledge I was bringing home a paycheck for a job I would have done for free. Most importantly, I felt like I was doing what I was supposed to be doing. I was being productive and creating enjoyable and entertaining content that would engage viewers. I loved the notion that I spent my entire day filming a movie and taking photos that others could enjoy. My sweat and labor had been put into this art. Erotica is rarely discussed in media and popular culture in the way that I see it—the way the performers see it. Porn should be elevated to what it is, an art form, and discussed for what it is, a complex genre of film.

This is the narrative I peddled most of my career. This was true. These are my feelings—however, I was leaving a big part of the truth out. Always trying to defend this industry that I loved so much was one reason I did that. Another reason was because I was in denial for so long about the bad. Good and bad coexist. They are not mutually exclusive, and this part of my experience in porn is just as important as the negative experience. They don't cancel each other out, and I am sick of hiding the fact that the adult industry can be a toxic place. For so long I never said anything because I wanted the good to be the whole truth.

The Bad

What I didn't realize at the time was that the first few male performers I was booked with were all very good-looking—that would not be the case for every shoot. Maybe that was because I had signed a three-scene deal with a popular men's site called Brazzers, and all their male talent were well-endowed and handsome. Or maybe it was a ploy to get me to want to continue doing boy-girl in the first place. I was booked for months just doing solo videos where I masturbated to the camera, which was awkward, because I had no other performer's energy to bounce off. There was no training on how to act during sex on film, so I referenced other women's videos to get inspiration. Imagine walking onto a job with no real preparation but your own research and life skills. When it came to my girl-girl scenes, Devon kept getting phoned by directors with notes that I didn't seem happy on set or that my scenes were low energy.

I remember him calling me before my first boy-girl sex scene. "You need to bring up the enthusiasm in your scenes, Tasha. The directors haven't been happy with your work, so you need to do well today," he said in a stern voice that instantly made me burst into tears. His opinion carried so much weight for me because I felt like he believed in me. Greg Lansky, a director for my first all-girl sex scene, wrote an entire blog post about how "Tasha is just a pretty face, not a talented performer." This constant criticism made me feel awful. I was in tears and sobbing the day of my big boy-girl scene, up until it was time to film. I was so beside myself that my makeup needed to be touched up from tears running down my face. At the same time, Devon's pimp-like behavior also made me strive to be the best performer I could possibly be, because I am a perfectionist. His fear tactics worked on me, and he knew it. Then he told me to hand the phone over to Jordan Ash, my male talent for the scene that day. "Jordan, do not hurt Tasha. Do not be rough with Tasha. She is new. If you rip her, I will be furious," he said in his thick British accent. *Rip me? What am I, a rag doll?* I thought.

Unbeknownst to me, Jordan had ripped numerous women's vaginas and injured them as a result of being too rough. Jordan appeared annoyed that Devon was telling him how to act and what to do. He begrudgingly agreed. "Devon, I'll do my very best not to hurt her, but I can't guarantee anything. My penis is big, and accidents happen sometimes." This was a curveball I just wasn't expecting. It was time to film *Anglin' for a Banglin'*, my first boy-girl scene. Why was I being spoken about like I wasn't even present?

I had a script given to me that day on set, which was stressful, because I was afraid that I couldn't memorize it in the amount of time allotted. That became the fear for me throughout my career, and the more I studied, the more anxious I became. The dialogue was misogynistic and perpetuated the stereotypes I had heard about before entering the adult industry. The more I think about it, the more I wonder if the reason we got our scripts the same day of filming a scene was to keep women from saying, "This is nuts! I demand to change it before I shoot for you."

Once I was already on set, it was difficult to advocate for myself, as there was no other person on my team. Not even my own agent, since his interest was of course money and job completion. After we ran through dialogue, it was off to shoot a blow job scene on the Las Vegas Lake, which I realized as we got closer was illegal, due to nudity and sex. This wasn't a moral issue for me, but public nudity comes at great risk—and in Vegas, that risk is jail. Many times in my career, I ended up shooting scenes that involved locations, plot lines, and sometimes acts that I wasn't consulted about prior to being on set. I'm sure you must be thinking, *Why didn't you just leave?* The pressure I felt to stay on set once I started my scene was intense. I didn't want to lose work or gain a bad reputation among directors, who all spoke with one another. Once I was even arrested in a Vegas hotel where we were filming a dialogue scene. The director hadn't pulled a permit. The porn parody of *Blue Velvet* was already making me uneasy; parodies are so cheesy. The police came in like I was committing some heinous crime for speaking on camera. I was handcuffed in front of everyone and couldn't stop freaking out, yelling and panicking because I was not expecting to be arrested at work. Yikes! I certainly never got into porn thinking it was a criminal activity.

The director, male performer, and I piled into a black SUV and drove out to the lake. "Tasha, are you dating Devon? You're a little thicker than what he normally goes for," Jordan, the male talent, creepily stated. Word traveled fast, and it was known to most that Devon dated the talent he managed.

I gave the blow job I was asked to perform on Jordan, with his huge cock in my mouth, on the boat in the middle of the water. Then we headed back to set in the studio. The scripted dialogue was silly; the plot line was about how my character had lost a fishing bet and then had to have sex with Jordan as the result. I always wondered who wrote these bizarre Brazzers scripts and why they would turn people on. Maybe most men feel less intimidated and therefore turned on by women who seem not as competent as them at a sport? I gave my all, swirling my hips around and around as I rode him reverse cowgirl, my least favorite position. I like to say, "It's the position porn made up."

I did not get hurt that day. I did learn that performing for a camera has little to do with the sex you have at home. As an entertainer, I want my audience to enjoy the moment. I want the camera to feel as though I love it. It is acting, even when it can be enjoyable.

Love Lace

I'll never forget my first Adult Video News awards show, at the Hard Rock Hotel in Las Vegas, Nevada, in 2010. I wore a pair of bedazzled True Religion jeans that screamed "These are expensive!" and a pair of super-tall nude heels right off Hollywood Boulevard. I had on a hand-painted blue-and-black crop top that must have cost me over five hundred dollars at Icara, a store that teetered right on the cusp of slutty and rich. Newport Beach was notorious for stores like that, which carried risqué outfits that you could imagine would be sold on Hollywood Boulevard for sex workers, but then priced outrageously and marketed to the wealthy women of Newport. I always loved these looks. In fact, I was always attracted to clothing that showed off my body. My mom encouraged that, even at a young age. I think it was her way of vicariously living through me, because she was forced to wear a uniform for twelve years of Catholic school and her mother's hand-sewn clothing on the weekends.

I had just lost ten pounds, which on me, being a whopping five foot four, looked dramatic. I wouldn't have even known that I had lost any weight at all, but while I was walking the convention floor, two of the most handsome male performers at the time exclaimed, "Wow, Tasha! You look great! You lost weight! You look like a different person!" I didn't even know I needed to lose weight until entering porn. Sure, I had heard modeling agents say I that could tighten up my belly. I had faced the rejection of Playmate of the Month from Hef himself and thought it could be because I needed to lose a few pounds. I had the pressure of maintaining my figure since before I could even remember, with my mother's voice saying loudly in my ear, "What are you eating?" while I dug through the kitchen pantry looking for snacks or dinner as a teen. My little sister and I read between the lines of this question to mean, "You've had enough food for the day; why are you consuming more calories?" I was raised in Orange County, and that is all I have to say to make most people understand the unhealthy relationship with my physical appearance that I had and still have today.

In all fairness, that video camera adds ten pounds and captures POV angles and upshots that are pretty cringeworthy if you are not used to being shot in that way. Due to stress, wanting to stand out, and casual criticism of my weight, I had restricted my food intake without even being conscious of it. Years later, in therapy, I would find that I had been practicing food restriction throughout most of my twenties without being aware of it. Eating disorders can be sneaky like that. Luckily mine was nothing to really write home over: no barfing, no full-blown starvation, just casual food restriction, where I would unconsciously skip meals or not eat a regular amount of food in order to lose weight or maintain my current weight. Sometimes it was money related, but honestly, I always had it in my head to watch what I was eating. Now I intuitively eat whatever the fuck I want.

There is a certain hierarchy in porn, and pretty privilege is part of that. If you're a seasoned performer and have built up your brand name, then you are at the top of the pyramid. But if you're a contract star, you're even higher up on the totem pole. A contract star is a woman whose performances are done only for one company. All her scenes are with that brand, under their umbrella, and her entire brand is enmeshed in the company itself. It is an honor to be asked to be a contract star, not only because the pay is better per scene but because it means that a big-name company believes in your star power enough and your personal brand so much that they want to work with you full-time. You have a guaranteed salary and regular appearances outside of movies, like signings. If you are a new and young starlet, you are above both tiers, but that title is short-lived, because you can only be new for so long, and there is a high turnover rate. There will always be a newer and younger woman coming along. At the bottom of the list are the "filler" girls, whom directors will book because their rates are low and they need more talent in the movie.

Directors will treat each woman differently depending on her place in the lineup and what they think they can get away with. For so long I was protected by Devon's intimidating reputation, giving me privilege in ways I didn't realize until it was gone. My whole career, I wanted to be a contract star. When that finally came to fruition, a series of unfortunate bosses came along with it. One owner of a production company would make sexual comments every time I came into his office and would sexually harass me any time he could. I had another boss who ended up getting sued for money laundering and stealing from his investors. It wasn't what I had envisioned, to say the least. I am not blaming the women of the adult industry; I just wonder who silenced their stories.

The women at the AVN awards came in all shapes and sizes. They were scantily clad, if not outright in lingerie, on the convention floor. Nudity was banned on the convention floor and security guards would demand that the models "Cover up your nipples!!" even though they were already covered by pasties. The Hard Rock Hotel was packed to the brim with mostly men and some women. Thousands of fans lined the hallways and the casino floor, just waiting for their chance to see or take a photo with their favorite actress. I had not been in many movies, so I wasn't signing (where you represent a company that you've shot movies for and sign your autograph) at anybody's booth. I was a mere onlooker, watching as the established performers sold their merchandise and signed autographs. I remember feeling on top of the world as random paparazzi, photographers, and fans would ask for a photo of me. I didn't hesitate to pose. I loved every bit of this action-packed fun. At age twenty-one, what was there not to love about the attention? I looked at myself in the mirror through my socialized male gaze, with my platinum-blonde extensions, my glowing spray tan, my perfect makeup, and thought, *Damn, I look good*. It was so fun to be able to see the biggest names in the industry and to mix and mingle with my coworkers. At nighttime, the convention took a turn in a different direction. I was invited to attend a *Penthouse* party, hosted by Jack Coe, the editor of the brand.

When I got into porn, Jack Coe owned *Penthouse* magazine. He was the CEO of Friend Finder, a very successful adult dating website, a producer of plays, and investor in many other companies. Jack was a multimillionaire who came off as an overall jolly, younger-looking version of Bill Gates. He was not intimidating but he had power—a unique find. I obliged. What took place next is a bit of blur. The food and liquor were poured generously. I recall dancing in exclusive nightclubs and being transported by limos and black cars. What I don't recall is who booked me to go home with one of his investors or friends. I truly have no recollection of the details, only knowing that my booking was sex-related and that I went to a man's hotel room after the club portion of my night. I was promptly paid out through my modeling agency. A fun night on the town with a little sex work.

Jack liked to party, and he partied hard. Soon after Vegas, he visited Los Angeles and invited me to his table with his other pretty *Penthouse* models. At this party, I was networking and socializing, but I had heard that if I wanted to a be a *Penthouse* Pet, the magazine's centerfold, I had to fuck Jack. It might seem strange, but at the time, this sort of quid pro quo was sadly common. I didn't think it sounded outrageous, especially because I had been in Hef's world with its many rules for so long. I just assumed that sleeping with the boss was now part of the work. The truth was that for every woman it was different. Some women slept with Jack and never became a Pet. Some women never had to sleep with him and became a Pet. But that night at the club, my peers implied that it was just something that happened.

I asked them, "What happens after the club? Do I go home with Jack and Karen [his girlfriend]?"

They giggled and said, "We're going home to our houses! But you have to party with them!" They were both already Pets and even a *Penthouse* Pet of the Year, so they had no pressure or obligation to really partake in anything they didn't want to do just to get the job.

The next thing I knew, I was piling into a black limo headed to the Mondrian hotel on Sunset Boulevard. If you ever need a shady place to conduct business, this is your spot. Karen, Jack's girlfriend, was much older than me, a brunette with a round face, maybe in her late forties. She was not attractive to me in any way, but she had an obvious crush on me. With no warning, she slid her hand down my pants and tried to finger my asshole. I was shocked, but I didn't want to blow my chances of centerfold. I was caught off guard and didn't reciprocate, which she soon noticed. She made some comment under her breath that I was just "too tight" for her finger. *I didn't sign up to hook up with her*, I thought, repulsed. This was out of my comfort zone.

That night I and many other women had sex with Jack in a title-motivated orgy, wanting to get crowned Penthouse Pet or hopefully Pet Of The Year. He swapped us around, and I tried my best to look like I was having fun. I will easily admit that when it comes to escorting, I was usually there for the paycheck and because it was something I was good at. I won't put up a façade and say I was ever orgasming or loving the physical work and labor of escorting. I wasn't. The good news was that sex with Jack was only for a short spurt of time. Because there were so many of us, it would have been hard to put his dick in all of us for more than two minutes at a time. I was hopeful that I was now a shoo-in for Pet, and I told Jack that it was a dream of mine to be centerfold for his magazine.

The next week, I was called into Devon's office. "I have good news, Tasha. You have been selected as *Penthouse* Pet of the month."

I squealed with delight. "Pet! No fucking way! I am so excited." Years at the *Playboy* Mansion, and never was I asked to be a centerfold. But now I had shoots lined up, a gold *Penthouse* key necklace that only Pets could have, interviews, trips—it was a big deal to me. Not only was I shooting as centerfold in one of the biggest men's magazines of all time, but there were many perks that went along with the job. I felt great about my career progression, even though I had slept with the owner for the position.

In the summer of 2012, Jack invited me to attend a gala with him and his new girlfriend, Marissa, in Monaco. I was allowed to bring my very best friend Brooklyn Lee with me, and we were both pumped. Her boyfriend, not so much . . . he was pissed. He was one of our agents at the time. He was very cocky and eccentric, racking up a list of performers he had dated or married. Brooklyn was his latest notch. We were flying first-class to one of the most magical places in Europe, and I made sure to bring a stunning green-and-blue floral gown from Neiman Marcus that I had borrowed from my girlfriend for the special occasion. It was a gala raising awareness and money to help with the environment—specifically climate change and all the damage it had done globally. The "A Night in Monaco" gala was for a good cause.

Once we got to Monte Carlo, we had to get ready as fast as possible in order to be on time for this party located at the Hôtel de Paris. Tired but young, I was ready for my close-up; at twenty-three years old, sleep didn't matter that much. When we arrived at the decadent dinner party hosted in part by former president of the United States Bill Clinton, I thought immediately that my mom would melt—she was a huge Clinton fan. On the way back from the ladies' room, I asked for a photo with Clinton. I caught his attention, and he agreed to the picture. My pose was a little sexy, I grabbed his tie and got close. I was stoked; I had gotten a sick photo for my memory box, and my mom would be proud.

A Night in Monaco was a star-studded event, and while I have always viewed the work that I did as a triple-X model and actress with the same respect and prestige as a mainstream model and actress, I quickly realized that I was alone in that. The photo went viral instantly. TMZ called Brooklyn and me to ask for specifics, but because we were twenty-three in Europe, we were also intoxicated. I yelled, "We're on a yacht, I can't hear you!" as the interviewer on the other line made fun of us. Our publicist had set up calls for us with press, but I was so aloof I didn't realize it was a negative thing.

The media spun a crazy narrative about Bill Clinton and me, since he already had a reputation based on the Monica Lewinsky scandal. Reporters, news outlets, and social media followers poured in, asking me about the circumstances surrounding the photo op. They implied I was his escort or some porn star slut who was seeing him after the dinner. The questions were dehumanizing, to say the least, and made me feel othered. I did not view myself in the way others seemed to be viewing me. I hadn't given much thought to that until this moment was trending on every news outlet internationally. I was defensive and on edge, answering questions about why I was at this exclusive dinner party, how I got a photo op with Clinton, and, more specifically, if I had seen him afterward. I was being slut-shamed for no reason at all, and all I could hear in the moment was "Why is a whore like you hanging out with influential, important people in Monaco?" It was heartbreaking, and I couldn't help but let it affect my self-esteem. I tried my best to come off as offended—because I was—and to start a conversation about why the attention over this topic was unwarranted. No one wanted to listen. When I signed at conventions, fans would bring the photo. When I did interviews, it was what everyone wanted to ask me about. I hated this sort of attention. I had never desired infamy. My stepfather reared his ugly head, asking my little sister to "Tell Rachel she sounds stupid on TMZ." I was twenty-three—of course I sounded silly, that's what your twenties are for.

At least the derogatory remarks and conversation booked me a job. "Digital Playground called. They want you and Brooklyn

Lee in a boy-boy-girl sex scene with Manuel Ferrara for the new blockbuster *Code of Honor*."

I was stoked. I always loved the opportunity to work for Digital Playground, and Robby D, the director I had met the first day I stepped onto an adult film set, was directing this movie. My male talent was gorgeous, talented, and I looked forward to my second time fucking him. My dialogue was light. I wasn't a contract star, so I was there for the sex. My bikini was green and gold, beach bunny swimwear, with a cute little white flower pinned on the right boob. I had finals at UCLA that week, so it was a rough time trying to finish essays and getting them delivered—in paper format—to my professors' mailboxes at UCLA on my lunch break. I was spreading myself thin, figuratively and literally.

After I did my pretty girl photos, I went into hair and makeup for touch-ups. At this point in my career, I was a strong performer, but I wasn't going to lose an eyelash while giving a blow job—that was for Brooklyn Lee. She was a Spiegler girl, which was a different brand of performer. Mark Spiegler was notorious for having the most extreme talent in all the industry. His agency was well-known, and it was a statement to be signed with him. Brooklyn was a hard-core performer who was rougher than most male talent I had worked with. To my dismay, Robby wanted a Brooklyn performance, not a Tasha performance. Immediately after starting hard-core sex, Robbie called "Cut!" What could I possibly have been doing wrong? Sure, it was 10:00 p.m. by the time we started our sex scene, and we had been there all day shooting visuals and plot, so everyone was wiped. That's the way adult sets operate, with no union regulating the hours and lots of hurry-up-and-wait moments.

"Tasha, you're not giving us the energy we're looking for. I want full-out, intense acting, like Brooklyn." I felt humiliated and ashamed, being scolded by this old bald man about my shitty sex skills.

I was even more bummed out when Manuel chimed in. "Tasha, just let go, let go. Stop getting in your head so much!" he said to me in a disappointed tone. Great, now one of the best male performers in the business thought I was a shitty lay. Could my night get any worse? Was I really that bad at sex? Or were they just ganging up on me? Either way, it really grossed me out to have to have sex with Brooklyn Lee, because she was like a sister to me. While in escorting, you can fake it and hope no one sees your facial expression, in porn it's difficult, because the camera sees everything. I got back into the scene and tried my best, even after that confrontation. My recoveries from altercations like this were getting quicker. Being on set is not for the faint of heart. It takes a strong backbone and thick skin to take the criticism and judgment that artists deal with on a regular basis.

The Patriarchal Bargain

"A patriarchal bargain is a decision to accept gender rules that disadvantage women in exchange for whatever power one can wrest from the system. It is an individual strategy designed to manipulate the system to one's best advantage, but one that leaves the system itself intact."

—LISA WADE

I was at the Mondrian hotel for a late-night meetup with the sister of my best friend. This rendezvous wasn't your average girls' night out. Penelope had specifically texted me because her sugar daddy, Justin, was a huge fan. Justin wanted to meet me, and Penelope wanted to make that wish come true. That was fine by me; after all, I was in my early twenties, and I was being paid thousands of dollars to party for under an hour. There would be champagne in a big suite at the Mondrian hotel. "Sounds great!" I texted her after she proposed the deal. The only catch was that part of the job was having sex with her and him together. He was an older man and not necessarily my type, but I had escorted before, albeit years earlier. Although it had been a while, I thought I could do it and make some quick cash. Devon had put a stop to me escorting once I signed with his modeling agency and was adamant I refrain from it while he and I dated. But now I was single. Daddy D didn't have to know.

Penelope mentioned, on the night that I had already committed to having a threesome, that she would be taking a cut of the money. I agreed, although I felt pressured to pay her, and went about my evening. Negotiating finances is something to be done before someone has committed to a job, not after. We arrived in his suite, and she really took charge of the seduction, which was nice. She made it all happen: the dancing, the entertainment—the whole vibe. I didn't think much of the interaction, except it was odd that I had fucked her sister so many times on camera. Also that she brought the topic of her sister up during the threesome that night. They worked together often. I don't know to what extent, but it definitely was a draw for clients. Her sister was a Playmate and had confided in me that she had posed nude for *Playboy* magazine while underage. I guess she had a great fake ID. Penelope was hot and the money was great, so overall it was a fun and productive night. However, I had no idea I was about to have a sugar daddy who was so invested.

The next morning, Penelope texted me to tell me that she wanted a cut from each time I saw Justin in the future. I agreed, but I should have been more up front and honest, because I had no intention of sharing my profits. She was not my madam and I was not bound to her, but I did want a consistent arrangement with Justin. After all, I was young and single, and being spoiled was something I desired.

He called me the next day. "Hey, Rachel, this is Justin! I would love to see you alone soon." Not thinking too much of it, I committed to our next date, which I believe is when he fell in love with me. The strange part of escorting is that the client can fall madly in love with you and the feelings are not reciprocated, but the service you're providing tells him otherwise. It really is an act of service and a kind deed for many men who want or need companionship. Justin was not an attractive guy, but he was charming. He was not tall, but he was charismatic. He was married to a blind woman who allowed him to seek companionship outside his marriage—or at least that's what he told Penelope. He avoided speaking about his family relations with me.

A typical date for Justin and me would be a fancy dinner wherever I wanted to go, an expensive shopping spree of my choice (usually WildFox or Louboutin), and then of course a bottle of Veuve Clicquot before playtime . . . until I stopped wanting to do that. I would just go shopping and tell him I felt sick afterward. Then I would return home to the condo he paid for in Brentwood. Justin ended up spoiling me so much over the next few years that I literally had to get him to write a letter to the IRS to own up to the $100,000-plus in gift money I had received. I sure didn't want to be audited for "gifts" I had earned during our time together. The government doesn't make escorting or sugaring or exchanging company for money easy in California.

I have never fully understood the resistance to legalizing sex work. So many women and men engage in it that legalization would only make the world a safer place for those who do. Taxes charged could take care of the uneven roads and disparity in education. Women could be more protected and men responsible for their actions. I've always thanked my lucky stars that I wasn't killed or kidnapped during my time escorting. The lack of regulation creates a perfect playground for someone who wants to commit senseless crime. The privilege I enjoyed working with agencies and high-end clients is probably the main reason I was safer than most, but unfortunately, I did experience some devastating interactions. Maybe one day I'll be brave enough to share it. I also know of an agency that has actual escorting contracts that outline that sex is not a guarantee and the client is accountable and verified. I've only ever heard of one person doing that in LA, and I heard about it after I stopped. I have a friend who was not only audited but arrested and detained for escorting. It seems like if you're making too much money from the career, then the IRS has a problem.

Justin let me have whatever I wanted. VIP at Coachella, as many Louis Vuittons as I wanted, meals at the best restaurants in all of LA, front-row tickets at any major sporting event or concert, VIP Super Bowl passes. . . . He spent thousands upon thousands of dollars on me each year. He showed me off by taking me back-stage at an intimate Coldplay concert to hang out briefly with Chris Martin. I was his date to a Kendrick Lamar concert; he paid me to record a voice-over for a Super Bowl commercial; I would visit his office; we were intimate. He loved taking me shop-ping and out on the town. He spared no expense and knew how to make me feel special. But there was a catch ... he wanted my heart. You can't buy love, and for that I was sorry. I was repulsed by Justin.

"Why don't you fuck me like you do the men in the movies?" he would ask me after we had a session.

"I'm sorry, but I'm just being myself. I'm not performing. Do you want me to perform like I'm being filmed, Justin?" I assume he was referring to lack of enthusiasm I would show in the bedroom. The pressure to be Tasha Reign was great and the stakes were high, but I was selling sex, so what did I expect? It was truly exhausting to escort. Sure, the lifestyle of wealth and opulence was enjoyable, but at what cost? I needed to be intoxicated to hook up with this elderly man. But it was fun having intellectual conversations with him, and I thoroughly enjoyed his brain. The last time I saw him, he met me in Arizona at some hotel so that I could collect VIP Super Bowl tickets. He hadn't asked me to visit or stay, so I wondered what could possibly have changed. I later learned at the game—he had moved on to another well-known, blonde adult film actress. She had better seats, sideline passes, and she let me know Justin was hers and I was—well, I was okay with that.

The Art of Feature Dancing

"You'll be feature dancing in Sacramento at Gold Club Centerfolds," Devon alerted me a couple months into my career as a porn star.

What is feature dancing, anyway? Feature dancing is a performance put on at a gentlemen's club by an adult actress. She headlines at the club, and her image is used to advertise and promote the weekend she will be performing. She is required to dance one to two sets or more a night. Those sets can be six to ten minutes long, and they can be elaborate or simple, but the goal is to be the highlight of that evening. You can imagine my shock when I realized this was a compulsory job on top of performing in movies.

I had danced as a house girl (a stripper) when I was nineteen and twenty years old in Los Angeles, but what was being asked of me of was much more demanding and intricate than dancing for a customer. I was asked to come up with a routine for at least two separate sets. I needed costumes and music and props. Why did it feel like I had to dance? I don't recall ever being asked if I wanted to dance. I must have just presumed that I needed to, because I had apparently already been booked to do it. That was like a lot of things in Devon's world; there was no gun to your head, but also, there was no conversation, and if I didn't do what he wanted, I wouldn't be a priority.

I picked out a cute black-and-white referee costume to dance to Too Short's song "Blow the Whistle," then a cowboy outfit to dance to Kid Rock's "Cowboy." In addition to these, I picked out some cute props, like a lasso and a whistle and a shiny blue rhinestoned...butt plug. I didn't know this was against club rules. Why would it be? I guess something to do with penetration. This gig required me to sign the few movies that I had been in at their

DVD and merchandise store for a few hours and then dance not two but *seven* different times in one night.

What a way to be initiated. It was exhausting: the entire performance, signing movies for fans afterward, even giving personal dances to fans—it was more work than I wanted to do.

Backstage is nerve-racking. My roadie was a real piece of work. I didn't hire him—he was assigned to me, and he was pessimistic and annoying. At the beginning of this job, I just went along with a lot of things I would end up questioning later, like having this glorified assistant assigned to travel with me. He even shared a room with me . . . in a separate bed, of course, but how uncomfortable and weird, like an unwanted babysitter I never invited. His duty was to collect my tips and arrange the sales of my product after the show, but he was talkative and creepy with the house girls, rarely helping me make more money.

They sent new performers out to an old, dusty club for small amounts of money so that they could practice the skills they would be encouraged to use every single weekend if the agent could book them that much. I ended up in this position, forever exhausted from traveling back and forth to Sacramento, Ohio, New York— you name it. It left me with the deep desire to never have to leave my house. That much traveling really wears and tears on you. The thought of the airport made me cringe. However, there was a reason why I kept getting booked and going back to the club scene.

There is a certain moment on stage that is extremely rewarding—a high, if you will. Yes, I always had a few Fireball shots before making a grand entrance on the pole, but there's a certain high you get from dancing. Even as a house girl, I felt the excitement. But as a feature dancer, you are the main attraction, and depending on what club you headline, you can pack in hundreds of loyal fans. The energy can feel incredible, like everyone is cheering you on, and you enter a trance that keeps you coming back for more. Not every night will be like this, but when that hits you, you want to keep coming back in hopes that tonight will be that type of night. For me, it wasn't even about the money; I loved getting to affect my fans and gain new ones. I felt that moment of ecstasy on occasion while I stripped down for everyone to see. I guess at heart I am an exhibitionist; it is deeply part of who I am.

Feature dancing will take a toll on your body and your soul. Physically, my kneecaps, legs, and other parts of my body are all damaged from slamming them onto the hard stage floor. Bruises were a given, but I feel the back pain to this day. Not to mention the emotional toll. I haven't danced in years, but sometimes I go to bed thinking of my time in the club and the environment, which caused me great distress and great pleasure. Like so many things in the adult industry, there is a side of dancing that no one wants to talk about it. Not your agent who makes money off you, not the club that profits from your show, and certainly not the patrons who are not exempt from touching you. That would be the sexual assault and harassment that so often occurs in the shadowy nights behind the "gentlemen's club" doors.

You know what I miss, though? I miss the music, the smell, the energy of a fun night at the strip club, as a stripper. I miss the mischievous dancers in the locker room and the different sweet perfumes filling the air. I love the energy of a good night, packed with fans and excitement. I miss Jessica, my favorite roadie, helping me get dressed to go on stage in a skimpy themed costume with music to match it. I miss meeting the house dancers in Ohio and hearing their life stories. I miss the cash being thrown over me on a stage when the audience is entertained. I miss that tired, achy feeling at the end of a long night that reminds me of how hard I worked and what a great show I put on. I miss the cash-stuffed suitcases and McDonald's drive-through at 3:00 a.m.

I don't miss the red-eye flights, the mostly cheap hotels (because that's all Canton, Ohio, has to offer), and I certainly don't miss the inappropriate work environment.

The Cock

I could write an entire book on male talent in this business and an analysis of their sacred position in the adult industry. Male talent are a pivotal and solid part of filmmaking, but they don't quite get the notoriety or the attention that the women in the business get. They're absolutely necessary and less replaceable than women, though. That's because their skill is so specific and so difficult, and there are not a lot of capable performers competing for this coveted position, simply because most men can't get hard on command, come in front of a room full of people when asked to, and open up to the camera by showcasing the female talent. That's a really specific set of skills to have.

There are few other professions where women get paid more than men because they are women, and I think that speaks largely to our societal values. Even today, it seems a woman's worth is often her beauty—not solely, but most importantly. I'm not complaining about making more than my male coworkers, but it certainly is food for thought. On average, my male coworkers would get paid starting from one quarter of my rate. They would only match it if they were the cream-of-the-crop performers. This hierarchy translates to on-set behavior and makes the male talent less threatening. Knowing that you, the female talent, are the highest-paid person on set is empowering, even in a world where many disempowering things could potentially happen on set. Some of my favorite male talent to work with I would call my on-set boyfriends. These were men I would always be paired with or whom I would see all the time, or talent I just loved working with. There is a certain comfort in knowing your scene partner. To know what to expect from the performance feels secure, and to trust the person you are having sex with is a reassuring feeling in a moment that is so vulnerable.

To really thrive as a male performer, you need to be able to get an erection on command. Unfortunately, some men must use drugs like Viagra or Cialis, or even shoot up their cocks with steroids, to make this happen. Others, usually the younger guys, are gifted and can get a hard-on naturally. Some talent can even ejaculate multiple times in a row. Having sex, coming, and then doing it all over again right after is impressive. Porn made me a size queen. It made my expectations higher in the bedroom, but sex work as an escort made me empathic. I have seen a lot of dick in my life, and I feel knowledgeable in an area where many people have unanswered questions. Being a porn star makes me the go-to girl among my civilian (people outside of porn) friends when it comes to questions about sex.

Often, directors will ask the male talent to arrive hours after the female performer, because we need time to do hair and makeup and pick out wardrobe. Simultaneously, it helps to keep the talent from clashing personally before they do the scene, which is something to be avoided. It is rare, but when talent clash on set before sexy time, it can lead to the entire day being ruined, money lost, or even violence.

Nacho Vidal is a well-known European performer who is famously recognized for his "strong" scenes. "Strong" translates into rough scenes in porn. I have always loathed that term, especially concerning male talent. "Oh, he's a strong performer," my agent Devon would say as he described male talent who were rough on set with their female counterparts. That is why I was shocked when Devon suggested that Nacho and I work together for our websites. Content trade is a common practice in the adult industry. There is a low overhead cost when talent trade their services to one another.

The bigger the name of the performer you work with, the better the traffic will be to your website, so I assume that my agent was just thinking in numbers and not keenly aware that Nacho was a violent person on set, before Devon sent me to our director Chris Streams's home. I certainly didn't realize the mess I was going to step into that day, so I packed my baby wipes, lingerie, and set bag and headed to the Valley. After a couple of hours of hair and makeup, Nacho arrived. He had an energy about him that was otherworldly, almost like a vampire. He confidently introduced himself as I was getting out of hair and makeup, and I was immediately turned off. This was rare. The trick about sex with strangers is that you must find something about the other person that is attractive. It could be their shyness, their earlobe, anything at all. You focus on that sexy or sweet attribute in order to convince yourself that you are into them, even for just a short moment in time. It rarely feels like a short moment, though. Porn time can feel quick or long, but never in between.

I went upstairs for pretty girl photos with the director I had worked with many times before, and as he started snapping photos of me, Nacho appeared. Normally the male talent doesn't watch me take pictures, but since it was for our own websites, it wasn't that weird. What was curious was the way he grabbed my leg and started rubbing it. If he was someone I had worked with before, maybe it would have been different. But my immediate reaction was repulsion, and you could it read on my face. As much as I am a good actress, in real life, my emotions are often obvious.

Surprise! Nacho had brought an accessory, a pair of black surgical gloves. What the fuck he was going to do with the gloves, I didn't know. I couldn't wrap my head around why he had them at all, let alone how he would use them in the scene. I said, "I am not comfortable with you wearing those in our scene," in a strong enough voice that I felt was assertive enough to stop him from forcing the prop on me. I was met with resistance, probably because he had a vision of the way the day was going to go, or maybe because he wasn't usually met with such reluctance. He angrily agreed and put the black gloves back in his bag.

Then he whipped out his dick for sex stills. I figured we would take them during the sex scene, but he wanted to do them prior. I went along with it, but as I got closer to his penis to suck on it for our photos, I gagged. The smell was awful—I couldn't do my job. I quickly got up and asked, with all the politeness I could muster, "I am so sorry, can you please go baby wipe your dick?"

I should have known what was coming next. "What the fuck? Who do you think you are? I'm not doing this fucking scene with you, you fucking bitch!" he screamed at me as he threw a remote control at my head. I ducked, and it hit the wall. I had never experienced this type of personality from a performer. Chris, the director, just stood there calmly as Nacho stormed down the stairs. I was shaken, I was scared, and I was confused. What had I done wrong? Couldn't I say what penis was going into my mouth?

Later that evening, I received an intimidating Twitter message from Nacho. "Don't say anything to anyone about what happened today." I brushed it under the rug and put him on my no list. This was my reaction to many inappropriate instances, because what are you supposed to do when you have a high-risk job in a business that will shame you for speaking out? I was just grateful that the fight didn't escalate further, that I was safe, and most importantly, that I didn't have to suck a poopy dick.

When you think of coercion, you often think of a frat party at some college, where booze is abundant and girls have gone wild. You might not think of sex workers who are coerced or pressured into positions they didn't fully realize they would be in. Or maybe you do . . . but chances are, you haven't heard many stories with that narrative. Society and our legal system often don't understand the nuances of rape and coercion in situations that aren't black-and-white.

The Money Shot

Anal sex. I wish I could say the rumors aren't true, that drugs aren't necessary to perform in risky sex acts on set, but I can't. I've rarely done an anal scene without taking a Valium I would get from my agent, and that goes for double penetration scenes, too. Double penetration is when a female performer is fucked in both the ass and the vagina at the same time, in the same scene. Both anal and DP scenes can be extremely overwhelming. I had never done either act before becoming a performer. Women in adult films take pride in the fact that they're able to achieve this strenuous act on camera. Remember, the men are well-endowed, the sex is hard, fast, and long. It is not for the faint of heart. I knew taking medication I wasn't prescribed was wrong, but I also knew that I couldn't physically stand the pressure and pain of anal sex without it. I had tried to practice with gradually increasing the size of dildos and had felt very uncomfortable. As a performer, you want to keep your audience interested and engaged, always giving them something new to look forward to. It had been years of vaginal sex only. I thought it was time for the butt stuff. Nobody had pressured me to do it, I just had this mind-set that I needed/wanted to give my fans more.

Anal sex is not supposed to hurt if done properly, prepped for correctly, and executed with patience. For me, it did hurt. I enjoyed orgasming with a penis in my ass, sure, but getting a porn-sized cock in there in the first place was a feat in and of itself. I know there are plenty of performers who can perform this act naturally, but I'm just not one of them, and I know I'm not alone. The first time I saw a woman chugging wine before a group anal scene, I thought, *That seems like an odd choice*, but then once I started figuring out my routine before an anal scene, I realized I, too, would need to use drugs to get through or enjoy my work. Once, on set for a strictly anal Cinderella-themed sex scene, I was caught red-handed with pills. I denied that I used them for the day, but an extra on set called me out in front of everyone. I went upstairs with the two men I was performing with that day. They were a sexy European duo who knew how to fuck on film and off. I had done plenty of scenes with them, but I had never done a DP scene in my life. I wasn't booked to do one that day, either. But I did quickly take the offer of trying out what it would feel like to have both men inside of me at the same time. I have a feeling the male performers like to brag about which porn girls they have fucked off camera. I was selective, but off-camera sex was always more fun.

Posing for print magazines was a highlight for me. Something about the glossy pages and the exclusivity of the print medium made me giddy. When *Hustler* asked me to test for the cover, I was beyond ecstatic. I had recently shot a gorgeous pastel photo set covered in tulle for Holly Randall, who submitted the photos for purchase. Instead, they booked me to shoot for them directly.

"Tasha, please remember to get your roots done!" my agency's front desk manager casually said. "Larry Flynt doesn't like roots on women . . ." I didn't think much of it, because my hair always looked good, and in Orange County, having straight bleach at the top of your hair was a symbol of "the 909," or the Inland Empire area of Southern California, which was less desirable. So, I didn't get my roots bleached but instead had a natural highlight per usual for the shoot. I showed up to set with a European photographer who kept asking me to push my butt up in the air for the cover shot. I had a great ass, and I knew it. We spent tons of time perfecting the shot, and I thought we got it. I had bright-red lips that day, and I felt a little like an unsexy clown. I don't care for a red lip. The pictorial theme that day was me as a hustler/thief who had stolen money from my lover, so there was money surrounding me and a briefcase of money I had stolen next to me as a prop. I had handcuffs and a skimpy black lingerie outfit. I embodied a *Hustler* model. That day I went home feeling accomplished and looked forward to seeing the photos one day.

One day came. I didn't make the cover of *Hustler*. Instead, they turned my photo shoot into one of the many pictorials in the magazine that month. Another letdown, but I was optimistic to see what the layout looked like. I only knew it was published because one of my loyal fans notified me, alarmed and upset, via Twitter. I immediately purchased the magazine and read the accompanying text.

About Tasha Reign

*D*espite *repeated attempts to contact Tasha Reign via tele-phone, email, and her talent agency, we were unable to acquire any personal information about the lovely assassin featured on these pages. Perhaps she is hard at work on another top-secret assignment. Regardless of the reason, we were forced to concoct a conversation with the elusive blonde. Under the circumstances, we did the best job possible.*

What's your hometown? "*I'd rather not give out too many details about myself. Say that I live somewhere in North America. Guys like that aura of mystery.*" *Do you enjoy traveling?* "*It depends. I don't like going to Europe, because over there I'm three inches shorter. It's got something to do with the metric system or the different gravity, but it sucks.*"

What was your most memorable sexual experience? "*Without a doubt, it was in high school. I came downstairs to get a glass of Tang, and my parents were making love on the couch. It was beautiful; their sagging, pale skin was bathed in the flickering glow of late-night porn on Cinemax. They went at it until dawn. I couldn't look away, even when my dad took a break to borrow anal beads from our next-door neighbor. Sometimes, when I need to feel extra-sexy on a photo shoot, I'll shut my eyes and recall that glorious night.*"

Do you have any sexual fantasies? "*I've always dreamed about participating in a mixed-bird gangbang. Pigeons, penguins, emus—whatever shows up.*"

Including ostriches? "*Of course not! Don't be fucking gross.*"

Is there anything else we should know about you? "*I enjoy watching lizards make love on a sidewalk.*"

Intriguing. Anything else? "No, you know plenty about me already. This has gone on long enough, hasn't it?"
Yes, Tasha, it has.

My heart sank. The author had said he couldn't get in touch with me in the "interview" that he made up, but I had no recollection of anyone attempting to get an actual interview from me. Even if I had let one of my many emails that year slide, did I deserve this sick and twisted story about my deceased father in a porn magazine? I think not. I was fuming, so I took my anger to the Twitter-verse to vent. I called *Hustler* out. "Why did you write this about me?" I angrily tweeted to their account. I just couldn't understand who had it out for me. Someone at the magazine ended up apologizing to my agent and, indirectly, to me. I learned my lesson that day: in porn you can't expect to control the narrative of your art. When you pose for someone else, you are leaving the editing and result up to them. They can do whatever they choose with the content, so be careful. I have now heard from a handful of models that they either were never paid for their *Hustler* cover or who, at eighteen years of age, had no idea that posing for photos for another company's website would land them on *Hustler*'s cover. They weren't even told their photos could be sold, or maybe they got into a bad contract. This is common.

I'm not scared of a big dick. After all, I have had some of the biggest penises in the world in my orifices. However, on a few occasions, I have been absolutely stressed about going to work on a set. The late Billy Glide was one of those cases. I came to set in 2011 ready to shoot some boy-girl porn. I didn't always look up my fellow performer's penis in the days leading up to a movie. Did I look at their face or even a quick video before we shot a movie? Absolutely. But I wasn't measuring cock sizes. On this day, the makeup artist had a worried look in her eye.

"Tasha, have you seen Billy's dick?" she asked me tentatively.

"Not in person," I said. "Why?"

She explained that he was more well-endowed than usual, even for porn. "Tasha, he's the width of a Coke bottle."

My mouth dropped, and my eyes bugged out. "A Coke bottle?" *Sounds alarming,* I thought. That would hurt, I assumed, and started to panic. The truth is, just because someone is well endowed doesn't mean they will necessarily be difficult to fuck or to fit into your vagina. It's all about the texture. Are they firm, like Johnny Sins? Or are they nice and squishy, like Mike Adriano? Billy Glide was nice and soft. Not limp, but just malleable enough to be able to get in the vulva without hurting. I was absolutely relieved to not have to face a painful day on set, or even worse, to have to go home because I couldn't complete the mission. The more you know . . .

The Fairy-Tale Dystopia

Everyone loves a fairy tale, especially me. In fact, I designed my whole house around a fairy-tale theme. However, I am a genuine and authentic person at heart, so the false narrative I had been peddling to protect myself had to come to an end eventually. Here is the fairy tale:

Once upon a time, there lived a gorgeous princess from Laguna Beach. She always wanted to be a model, and she discovered a niche that was perfect for her and followed her dreams. She moved to Los Angeles and sought out work. She modeled for *Playboy* and secured one of the best agents in the adult business. She worked hard, traveling the world, signing autographs, making movies, and feature dancing. She loved her job and her fans so much that she had no complaints about it! In fact, she loved it so much that she stayed in the industry for over a decade and loved making scenes with all her scene partners.

Tasha Reign is such an advocate of the adult industry that she can't imagine how other people looking in can see it as exploitative. Especially because she is so empowered and went to years of college for an undergrad in women's studies and a master's degree in specialized journalism. She comes from a wealthy family and chose to do porn, dispelling the age-old narrative that women in sex work are forced into it. Tasha is a feminist and Tasha loves the adult industry! Xoxoxo

For almost a decade, I felt the need to maintain the fairy tale story for interviews, articles, and the press. Whether meeting fans at AVN or talking about the adult business to journalists, I had not broken my story. For a good reason, too. When you're a female performer in adult film, you are constantly attacked and put down by news outlets and society. In order to cope with this immense judgment, you become defensive. So defensive that you overlook issues that are happening to you, for fear of perpetuating unfair stigmas and stereotypes that are not true or misunderstood. If there was more room for nuance and less judgment, the pressure to maintain the façade wouldn't be so overwhelming. Over the years, with the help of the #MeToo movement, I finally felt empowered to speak out and speak up. With the influence of powerful women in Hollywood speaking out about the sexual harassment, assault, and rape they endured on mainstream sets and with mainstream directors, I found it suddenly perfectly acceptable to disclose the truth about what was happening on film sets in the porn world. To my dismay, it felt like the media cared less. Not that they didn't care at all, but that they expected it on a porn set. It was a very disappointing realization to have after risking my career and speaking out publicly about the predators behind the cameras.

The reality was grayer. People cared, the industry cared, fans and consumers and media outlets cared, but because we had no federally recognized union, change was difficult to implement. In addition to not being unionized, power players in the adult industries didn't want to believe or own up to what was happening for fear of having to change the business, implement safety protocols, and ultimately take responsibility. It was easier to deny it or to shame the performers who stood up. And for me, in 2018, that is what happened.

I'm not the first model to have had an emotionally abusive relationship with Devon Roy, and unfortunately, I won't be the last. At the time, I didn't bat an eye at dating my modeling agent. Why would I? It meant I would not only be favored, but that my career would be accelerated. I didn't realize it was unethical. Twenty eleven was long before the #MeToo movement, and I had no idea that I could be exploited, manipulated, or even coerced. I had the confidence of a twenty-one-year-old. Devon is a powerful man. His power comes from his ability to secure some of the best models and performers for adult film. It also comes from his ability to be cunning and manipulative to the point of coercion. It's difficult to admit, because at one point Devon was my boyfriend, my close friend, and a strong agent whom I credit my career and star power to. I'm a victim of coercion, which can feel like a trope. But I am also empowered by sex work. These two things are not mutually exclusive. American culture so badly wants to put women in boxes that it can feel like you must choose one or the other, but both can be true.

I heard rumors about Devon from the day I laid eyes on him. While on a trip to Star Island in Miami to shoot content, I had an overwhelming desire to work with Ben English, Devon Roy's alter ego. Ben English had been in over one thousand adult films. Ben English was hot, and Ben English had a big dick. I sought out Ben English without thinking of any of the consequences.

"Ouch!" Devon pulled hard on my hair from the back as he shot his warm load at my face, getting semen into my eyes so I couldn't even open them if I had wanted to. He was so rough, probably used to performing in the eighties— a different, rougher time period. I was spent. It's not always clear whether ejaculation into the eyes is intentional or not, but either way it hurts. It's as if the sperm thinks that the eye is an egg inside the fallopian tube, and it feels like the sperm is trying to penetrate your eyeball. It was my first time where that occurred on set, and I was startled. Even in the video, I look shook. I immediately went into the bathroom to cry. It was traumatic because he was my agent. Why had I wanted to shoot with him?

A co-worker of Devon's texted me right after. "Do you want to go to Boa with us?" Karen asked. I didn't want to go to share a meal with Devon and the rest of them, even at a nice restaurant. I felt violated. When I tried to state that, it got right back to Devon. I apprehensively accepted the invite because I felt pressured. From there on out, I was attached to Devon at the hip. At dinner, he made it clear to me that he didn't want me escorting. He was protective of me in some nontraditional way that my twenty-one-year-old self was attracted to.

Over the next few weeks, he quickly asked me to be his girlfriend. I obliged.

He could make me feel like I needed him to survive. He was also an agent who could make your star rise in the adult world. Devon is not a good man. He will take all he can and push you to do all you possibly can do and more. Despite everything I know about Devon, there is still love in my complicated feelings for him. I know—so cliché.

#MeToo

*"Other than grabbing my ass against my will, underneath my
skirt, and refusing to let go, he did not otherwise touch me
inappropriately."*

—TAYLOR SWIFT

A tall, tan, brunet man who bore a resemblance to Jesus Christ
lived directly across the street and one property up from the house
I lived in as a child, tucked away in a little apartment. His windows
had his curtains pulled wide open while he enjoyed having sex in full
view of everyone on the street. Children lived on our street, including
me. Steve was an acclaimed guru who was well-known and well-liked
internationally. He was successful in many areas, publishing popular
books, traveling the world with other spiritualists, and leading meditation ceremonies and retreats. He had a charismatic way about him
that made my mother trust him and accept his neighborly friendship.
He often waved at our little girls-only family from across the way.
Once my mom drove by his window while he was roughly fucking a
petite Asian woman who looked too young for him on a chair. The
chair had been placed in that spot in order to display the action. He
was clearly a weirdo, and this was his stage.

"Rachel, Steve is fucking that young woman's brains out in his window! He waved at me as I drove by—he must love everyone watching him fuck!" my mother exclaimed to me one afternoon. Her boundaries were nonexistent. I was only in middle school.

Steve used to take pictures of me and my girlfriends playing in the street. He was very nonchalant about this and kept the photos in his office in his home, even showing them to me on one occasion. He fancied himself a photographer. I told my mom about the photos, and she didn't flinch; she knew Steve. One day, he invited my girlfriend Candice and me into his place when we were twelve years old, to read our horoscopes. We were enthralled. We had little knowledge of fortune-tellers, but at the time it was very popular for girls' brands like Wet Seal and Limited Too to sell horoscope-labeled clothing. That day, Candice was wearing a shirt that said "Pisces." We were fooled by his charm and believed he could psychically guess when she was born. When we got home and figured out he had simply read her shirt, we were very annoyed seventh graders.

When I was fifteen, I started to dabble with mixing stolen prescription drugs with alcohol. I loved mixing Ambien with that sweet blue Hpnotiq bottle of hard liquor. The combination made me feel free of worry or anxiety. Unfortunately, it had other people worried about me. One night Candice and I walked down to our local Chinese restaurant, Mandarin King, and we sat down for dinner as usual. I felt loopy because I had dosed myself with this combination of drugs. Then I passed out in the green leather booth inside the restaurant. Candice announced to the restaurant I had taken the wrong medication and was having an allergic reaction, because she didn't want me to get in trouble. She rushed to pay our bill and helped me hobble out of the place as soon as I came to.

I wasn't in a good mental space. Steve was randomly on the road outside, and he got me home with Candice because he happened to see us struggling up our steep hill. Shortly afterward my mom told me I would be going to lunch with Steve. I'm not entirely sure if my mom reached out to Steve for help or if Steve reached out to my mom because he was worried, but Steve took me out for lunch at a café called Anastasia. He lectured me about drugs and asked me if I was being safe. He seemed truly concerned but mostly just talked to me as a friend. I didn't think it was creepy, as I felt mature at fifteen years old. Why would it be weird to be going to lunch with a fortysomething neighbor? After all, my mom approved of it.

I had known Steve all my life, so when I was twenty-one years old and Steve invited me over to his apartment to talk, I didn't think much of it. "I've seen your nude work online. Do you know I take photos, too?" he asked. He proceeded to show me his collection of all the nudes he had taken over time. I even recognized the woman in the window. He asked if he could take my photo.

"No, Steve, I really only want to shoot nudes for *Playboy*," I stated. He seemed sad but understood. If I was going to continue to pose for *Playboy*, I wasn't allowed to pose for other people or companies; that was a rule. It took me until now to understand how creepy it was for Steve to ask in the first place.

The next time I saw him, almost a decade had passed. He looked unchanged, still handsome. This time I had reached out, because I had recently been indoctrinated into transcendental meditation, and who better to ask for help than a real-life, certified yogi? TM is the practice of meditation, twice a day for twenty-minute intervals. You are given a sacred word and do a workshop in order to be a part of the David Lynch foundation, which I had been invited to join. Steve seemed short on cash this time, because he didn't offer to help with the parking fee. I treated us to one of my family-owned restaurants, 230 Forest Avenue, and we chatted. We took a stroll down memory lane. Then, in the cringiest way possible, he said, "When you were a little girl, you were always flirtatious with me, even from a young age. You've always been a vixen, Rachel." I couldn't believe he felt comfortable confiding this in me. He further went into detail about how my "free" porn videos were all over the internet and there were tons of them to view, then rambled about the #MeToo movement and how he was constantly being accused of harassing women in yoga and meditation.

I tried to follow up with, "Really? Women accused you? What did they say you've done?"

He was quiet and changed the topic quickly. Like so many predators, he had no empathy for his accusers, and there was no paper trail online to prove what he had done. When lunch was over, I was left with a sick feeling in my stomach. He offered to metaphorically or magically "install" a button in my head to press and connect to him in the future while he led us in a fifteen-minute meditation. I agreed and closed my eyes. That was the last time I saw Steve. But he was far from the only predatory man I would know in my life and in my career.

Deal With the Devil

Devon Roy had a funny way of tricking his models into doing work he foresaw them trying to refuse by leaving critical information out. In 2022, Devon got indicted as part of a criminal case for "conspiracy to commit pandering" and "conspiracy to commit pimping"—a case which has yet to go to trial as of this writing. He was accused of sexual assault by multiple performers. Adult stars claiming he raped them, assaulted them, or coerced them into work. He was arrested. I was not one of the women who spoke up.

The buildup to this was years in the making. The industry was not surprised at the accusations, but many were instead relieved that people were finally getting the courage to speak out against the agent. Everyone in the adult industry for the last twenty years has in some way or another been intimidated, scared, or personally bullied by Devon Roy. He is like a mobster in the porn industry. He knew the ins and outs of how to manipulate, and then applied them to his job as a modeling and movie agent in the business. I was no exception. For almost my entire career, I kept my blinders on and wouldn't accept the truth no matter how many times I was affected. No matter how many models told me their horrific stories, I wouldn't believe it. I even promoted his agency and services. I live with that now.

I dated Devon, I loved Devon, and I would even go as far as to defend him year after year. After all, he made me a star, put food on my table, and treated me "differently" than all the other models, giving me special attention and taking a noticeably serious interest in my career. In addition to work-related benefits, he would often accommodate my requests. He would give me references or connections to helpful people to further my brand. An account of all the times Devon took advantage of me would fill up a novel, but there are a couple of memorable accounts of trauma that will only take a chapter.

One morning, I was booked to shoot with a gorgeous Black woman named Skin Diamond, one of the industry's prettiest faces and strongest performers. There was no mention of race play, which involves participants acting out racially charged scenarios, when we booked or confirmed details over the phone and email. Devon knew I was openly antiracist. To confirm this story, I went through my old emails from LA Direct Models to see what the shared details about the shoot were: Skin Diamond, a director who has directed for a variety of things, the location in downtown Los Angeles at an industrial warehouse, and absolutely no mention of an emphasis on the fact that Skin Diamond was black and I was white.

As I got into hair and makeup, something about the set seemed sketchy, and the way the cameraman, who was filming an unusual amount of behind-the-scenes footage, was talking to Skin was demeaning. Both the director and the production assistant were acting as though her newly shaven head was in some way not attractive or not right for the shoot. It didn't sit well with me. *They don't pay us enough to control our haircuts!* I thought as these assholes berated her. I spoke up and said, "Hey, stop talking to her like that!" when they continued to make comments about her shaven head.

Women of color are treated worse than white women on most sets. Not all sets, but definitely in this case, this director's seedy set. You could imagine my shock and horror when I realized that the site Skin and I were supposed to shoot for was called Zebra Girls, with an emphasis on white-on-Black lesbian sex. The actual name is not that alarming, but when I took a deeper dive into what company owned Zebra Girls, I was jarred. It was none other than Dog ***** Media. That's right. Dog ***** is the actual name of an actual company in porn. They specialize in extremely degrading race-play pornography.

What the fuck! I thought as I dialed Devon's cell phone.

"Yes, Tasha, what is going on?" he said, annoyed, on the other end of the call.

"Did you know I was shooting a race-themed scene today?" At this point in my life, when I got to set, it was often too late to turn back. The #MeToo movement hadn't happened yet, so I was not emboldened enough to stand up for myself after committing to a job.

"Tasha, complete the scene and we can talk about it afterwards," Devon said, sounding stern. There was no fighting this.

If I didn't want to pay the break fee Devon was going to charge me for leaving, I was going to have to shoot this scene. Not to mention, I would be taking away Skin's check, my check, and the rest of the crew's checks for the day. The embarrassment I would have to suffer or Devon's anger didn't feel worth the energy it would take me to muster the courage to walk off set, but I would soon learn I had made the incorrect decision . . . a decision that haunts me to this day.

As Skin and I got ready for our lesbian sex scene, we tried on lingerie to make sure it coordinated with one another, picked out sex toys to use, and went to the director for approval, as usual. When I turned around just like he asked me to, this person who was my boss for that day slapped my bare ass hard. *Whack!* I was shocked and disgusted. This loser clearly got off on humiliation. He had, unbeknownst to me, been sued many times for nonconsensual forced racism toward performers during their scenes. He couldn't get at me that way, since I am white, so he used his next best move—sexual assault.

"What the fuck are you doing?" I screamed. He looked surprised that I had a response.

"I am sorry for molesting you," he said. I am haunted by the way he admitted molestation like that. At this point it's challenging to put my finger on why I didn't call 911, leave, call Devon, and tell him I was assaulted, but I was too scared. I was scared the director would get angrier, I feared what could happen next, and I was just mortified.

"What the fuck! That's not okay," I said. Skin just stared at me, not knowing what to do, either. The situation was toxic; it was everything about porn that I hate wrapped up into one shoot, and I felt frozen. The shame that came over me then and comes over me now as I type is crippling. Being the victim of sexual assault is never the victim's fault, but it sure as hell feels that way.

The message women have heard through media, their parents, patriarchal society—"You asked for it"—is difficult to shake. I don't know if you're ever really free of it.

Why didn't I leave, you ask? I asked myself that same question over the many times I was assaulted or harassed or coerced on set or at work. The answer is complicated, but ultimately, I didn't feel able. Some directors have gaslighting down to an art form, and this guy was a master. I tried to shake off the horrible way I felt and just power through the mess that was about to take place. The toys he wanted us to use were physically too big for us to put in our bodies. The craziest part of this whole story was that somehow, he got us to perform anal on one another, and that wasn't even the scene I was booked for. Anal is double. It was as if slapping me hard somehow put me into a trance where now anything abusive went and I had to tolerate it. I had never done acts that I wasn't going to be compensated for. I don't know what came over me. I was confused when Skin acted as though the toys were too big for her butt; now I realize that she was merely trying to get through the scene without another violent interaction from the director.

On a break, Skin and I noticed a colorful blue butterfly flying inside the warehouse, scared and alone. I immediately empathized with the beautiful, fluttering, trapped creature. Skin found a glass jar and together we caught her. I looked at this beautiful animal that God had created, to be free, to fly to live under the sun and moon, to enjoy life on her on terms and not to ever be trapped in a shitty warehouse in downtown LA. We freed her, to fly and live and not feel the fear of never being able to leave that dungeon of a stockroom. She was now back where she belonged, where I yearned to be that day on set—free.

To make the day even more traumatic, at the end of our scene we had to record "consent" videos with the predatory director.

"Were you treated well on set today?" he asked, like evil Jafar from *Aladdin*, trapping his hypnotized king.

"Everything's great!" I responded, trying to sound bubbly in order to hide my fear of this sicko. *I'm lucky I wasn't abused more today*, I thought.

"Hold up the DOG **** sign!" he demanded, and we obliged.

Skin retired shortly afterward. It was her last scene. I stayed silent about this incident for years, and then when #MeToo broke out, I wanted so badly to speak up, to do something about the damage that director had caused me that horrible day. The lawyers told me that the statute of limitations had passed, and I had no case, which is the sad truth about so many sexual assaults on set. By the time you are emotionally ready to take the case to court, the time is up and there is no chance. When I spoke to Skin years later, she mentioned that day was her last shoot.

A Flashback to Shame

When I was in fourth grade, I got called into the principal's office after school. I had no idea why I was there or how I'd ended up in trouble yet again. Trouble seemed to follow me everywhere I went, but I couldn't figure out why. "Are you aware that your daughter has hickeys on her neck?" the principal asked my mom. I had been playing in my father's hot tub with my stepsiblings, and they had experimented with giving me hickeys on my neck. They were four and three years my senior. Immediately I felt like I had done something wrong, like I was being personally shamed for having hickeys on my neck. This type of sexual shaming was just the beginning of me being blamed for things that other people did to me. It's the strangest thing, being a girl; adults make you feel bad about other people touching you, rather than talking to the people who did the touching.

When I was fifteen, I went to Cabo Club Med, Mexico, with

my father and his wife, as well as my three stepsiblings. I shared a villa with my older sister, and we had the freedom to set our own schedules. She met a tennis instructor, and I met Miguel, a local who was also on vacation.

Miguel was twenty-three. He hung out with my dad and me, kayaking in the sea with us during our stay. He was cute and flirtatious, and I was so attracted to him. He was also a pedophile. He's the first man who ever sexually assaulted me. He kissed me all the way down to my pants and slowly pulled them off. I had never had sex before and didn't know about the socialized millennial gender norm of a shaved vulva yet, which I would soon adhere to. *If I knew we were doing this, I would have shaved.* I trembled innocently. He looked me in the eyes and then ate me out. He swirled his tongue, bringing me to orgasm quickly. I had never felt anything like it. Did I enjoy it? Sure. But I was a child. I went about my trip, dining, shopping, and having fun with my family members. I loved hanging out with this adult man, and nobody seemed to care.

Years later, when I was twenty-two, I got an email ping from Miguel, through a fan account online, listed on my social media accounts. I was surprised and repulsed. I immediately responded, asking his age, so I could make sure it wasn't just in my head. It wasn't.

"I stumbled across you on the internet (hehe) and decided to shoot you an email after becoming a fan. I met you a few years back (like ten) at the Club Med in Ixtapa, Mexico. I don't know if you remember me, however, I wanted to say hi. Saw you were coming to Columbus, Ohio next week and wanted to know you have one longtime fan haha."

My heart dropped. I had never thought of myself as someone who had been molested, but confronting this dark memory a decade later, it felt like I had been. How many other women did this happen to? How many other women felt like they enjoyed a sexual interaction at the time, but only recognized the abuse years later? Probably a lot. I was left with an empty feeling in my stomach and an unseen title in my head—*damaged goods*. I didn't want to think that way about myself, but I had always heard this stereotype perpetuated about women who work in porn: "Oh, they must have been touched or molested." I had always thought that was bullshit. So, once I recognized that Miguel had molested me, I was saddened and confused. Had I been telling myself lies this whole time? Was I really part of this fictional tale that everyone had tried to push on me? Or was I now feeling the stigma of the societal box I had dreaded being squeezed into for so long?

I had been molested, but so have millions of women all over this country, continent, and world, and they hadn't "turned to porn" in order to cope with their trauma, and neither had I. I was sick and tired of society telling me how to think of myself. It's the absolute most challenging part of being an adult entertainer: controlling your narrative. It's challenging to speak your truth and have conviction in your choices without believing other people's harmful and negative misconceptions. Many survivors of sexual assault never say anything about it. I refuse to be one of them.

Years later I was in Ohio, doing a feature-dancing show at a club, and I was asked to go on a local radio station. As usual, I agreed to the booking and promoted my weekend appearance as much as possible. I always wanted the clubs to be packed with fans and customers so that they would want to hire me back and so they would be satisfied with their booking. After all, they were shelling out thousands of dollars as an investment in me and therefore their club, so I wanted to give them a return on their investment. I loved the notoriety I got on the club circuit. I grew to be one of the most-booked models and popular feature dancers, someone the owners and managers could rely on to show up on time and do a great job.

On the day of the interview, I woke up bright and early and headed on over to the radio station in a black car they sent for me. When I arrived, I was greeted by a shock jock. I hadn't really understood the concept of a shock jock before, but I learned immediately that I didn't like this guy's attitude. By the time the interview was over, I was ready to leave. But as I tried leaving the station, the man followed me out with a cameraman. "So, were you touched at a young age or were you fondled? Why is your voice so high? Isn't it true that most porn girls are victims of rape as children?" he barked at me as I looked back at him, wide-eyed and confused.

He didn't hesitate for one second to ask me these totally inappropriate questions. This man had clearly been taking advantage of women, specifically sex workers, and no one had ever put him in his place. I conducted the interview with fear in my eyes and tried to be as articulate as I could be. The video went viral on Reddit right away. Thousands of negative comments about this pervert of a man looking like a complete fool gave me some closure. I pushed the bad memory to the back of my mind. I had no reason to dwell on him or his bad behavior. But it would be far from the last time I was treated like an object instead of a person. Why do people feel like they are entitled to entertainers? People feel like they are entitled to entertainers' time, bodies, and attention. Maybe that is because they've seen what they consider the most intimate part of the performer and therefore they now feel like they know the performer? Or is it perhaps that society tells men that if a woman is a whore then you can disrespect her because she is not pure or chaste? Social media makes people feel close to complete strangers by allowing a virtual interaction that they wouldn't have otherwise, often getting a glimpse into entertainer's private lives. Ultimately, I don't think any of this is an excuse to treat any person with the disrespect that sex workers are so often treated with. Do you?

"This is Devon. Please call me." I received semiregular texts like this that sent chills through my body. It either meant my agent had booked me for a photo or video shoot . . . or that he needed to discuss something he was upset with or confused about. Devon has lived here in Los Angeles for thirty-plus years, and the fact he never lost his English accent is telling. It shows the type of person he is: stubborn.

"Tasha, Stormy would like to book you for November 15 and 16 as the lead in her new comedic movie, *The Set Up*." Butterflies fluttered in my belly and excitement ran through my head. Being the lead in a Wicked Pictures film was a big deal to me, as these roles were often reserved for their contract stars. To have the legendary Stormy Daniels direct the movie was even better. Stormy was a performer, contract star, director, model, and mother. I had looked up to her for years. In high school, she was the first adult film star I had seen in a documentary on television. I thought, *Wow, what a bad-ass boss!* as I watched her on my couch. When Devon told me about the role, I tried to play it cool because I didn't want to appear starstruck or shocked that she had booked me, but actually, I was both. She had chosen me, and that meant a lot.

Sure, I had signed autographs at the same booth at conventions as Stormy Daniels, danced at the same strip clubs, and I had even chatted with her multiple times, but for her to cast me as the main actress with lot of lines in her project was a milestone. I packed for set that day with lots of cute wardrobe options and made sure to have a fresh face for hair and makeup application. Hair and makeup, or "glam," can take anywhere from an hour to two hours, and you want to be a blank canvas so that the artist can do their job.

The makeup artist kept talking about how the stigma of porn stopped her from meeting eligible men. I had heard this sentiment repeated many times by fellow performers and by creatives in the industry. I had even complained about how the misunderstanding of the adult industry wore on me. But at this moment in time, I felt the real issue was internalized misogyny. The hardest part of being in the industry is the way people outside the business perceive you. Trying to actively avoid being the character projected upon me had become tiring.

Immediately upon arrival, Stormy and I got to chatting about the red carpet at the AVN awards a couple months prior. AVN is by far the adult industry's biggest award show, and it's considered one a true honor to be nominated. She was complaining that her costar jessica drake was too liberal, and she didn't want to be photographed next to jessica because she was wearing a faux burned American flag wrapped around her body as a message to President Donald Trump. She had just marched in the Women's March against corruption of his government and abuse of power regarding immigrants, the rights of sex workers, for black lives matter and the LBGTQ community. He had stated that anyone who burned the American flag should lose their citizenship and be thrown in prison.

I agreed with Stormy, because I am a patriotic person myself. *I wouldn't pose next to someone who would wear a burned fake American flag* . . . After all, even if I empathized with jessica, which I secretly did, I certainly wasn't going to voice a political opinion against my director. Directors have a lot of power.

Porn can often feel like a comedy set. People don't take themselves too seriously; they think of themselves as entertainers, which can be fun. The problem is that porn is not a comedy set. It is a sensitive place for some people and certainly a place where performers should be treated with care and respect. Showing up to a film set is not easy. You don't know exactly what you're getting into. You don't know who is going to be there. As Tori Black once said at an intimate dinner, "You want to know either the director or a performer on set." To know neither can be intimidating, or even dangerous. Luckily for me that day, I knew both.

The conversation got dark when a couple of the crew members started cracking jokes about Stormy being a Harvey Weinstein. Stormy herself admitted that she was physically and verbally flirtatious with a PA or a camera guy who was working for her, and that she tied him to his chair. I laughed because it was uncomfortable, but I also didn't want to get into a whole explanation of why the power differences and gender inequalities weren't comparable. I just swept it under the rug like so many other days on set and tried to get ready for my dialogue scene.

Stormy Days Ahead

I had heard Stormy was a real bully if you forgot the lines. I rarely had a lot of lines. I more often had sex-driven scripts than dialogue-driven scripts, so I was nervous. The movie was filmed over two long days. The adult industry doesn't have a union like mainstream SAG. Sadly, we as performers are not paid overtime or compensated when we arrive at 8:00 a.m. and leave at 3:00 a.m. any more than if we left at five p.m. We are just expected to show up, be grateful we are working, and not complain about it. It was one of those days.

I had two sex scenes and a few dialogue scenes to get finished within the forty-eight hours. I got to go home and sleep in between. My two separate sex scenes, with two awesome male performers I knew, were scheduled with one on each day. The first scene went swimmingly. I knew my dialogue, and my pretty-girl stills and box-cover photos were fabulous. I was having a good day. I enjoyed sex with the male talent, Seth Gamble, whom I had previously worked with at least a dozen times and had even flown to Japan with. We were like dancers in a routine that we knew very well. The angles, the shots, the sex; all of it was so warm and familiar. I loved my sparkly pink rhinestoned Skye dress, and my hair and makeup were on point.

I recognized several men on set, who were talking down to Stormy and joking around with her. I noted how rude their behavior was, but I was just there to get my job done and have some fun, so I tuned out their distasteful banter. Bad language, inappropriate sexual jokes, lots of laughing around the serious matter of Harvey Weinstein were all things I was offended by but sadly not surprised by. Being on set can be unpredictable depending on the crew. Some crews are feminist, some crews are just trying to get the job finished, and some crews are inappropriate. Like a recipe, what you add to the mix matters, and the taste comes out differently depending on the ingredients.

The day wrapped late, around two the next morning, and I headed home to rest up for the following day's early call time. Wicked sets are known for wrapping late after extremely long days. I felt good about the production and my acting. I was missing an industry event that I had helped plan to shoot this movie, but it was worth it, because I was shooting top-notch content that I was sure to be nominated for during award season.

I woke the next day feeling rested and ready to shoot my last scene in *The Set Up*. I drove myself to set, casually chatting with my girlfriend on the phone about how exciting the project was, and then went through the process of hair and makeup just as before. I shot whatever dialogue I needed to get out of the way before the sex scene. I posed for the pretty-girl photos and potential box-cover shots and continued with my character, Tasha Reign, just as I had the day before.

My paperwork hadn't been filled out for that day of filming yet, or for the day before, for that matter, and a production assistant reminded me that it needed to be done. He handed it to me to fill out after I had taken my solo photos for the upcoming sex scene. There are endless photos taken on set. I changed back into the skimpy outfit that was my designated costume for the scene I was about to shoot. Then I propped the paperwork up on a table nearby.

That's when I was sexually assaulted.

A cameraman I had never met or noticed before came up behind me and said, in the creepiest tone possible, "Oh yeah, baby, mmm, yeah . . ." while firmly groping my ass from behind. My heart sank. I knew instantly that this was not my costar Michael Vegas. I had been openly harassed and assaulted at work. Not just on any production set, but on a set run by arguably the most professional company in the adult industries. And it wasn't someone I knew, but a random crew member. I wasn't alone, either. I was in a room with open doors near many other people. It wasn't the sex on set that was an issue in porn, it was the culture.

My stomach immediately hurt, and I felt sickened. I called out the camera guy right there and then, saying, "WTF are you doing? Why did you do that? What is wrong with you?" He wandered off into some corner. People on set wanted to know why I was so angry, but I was about to do my sex scene. I couldn't cry off all my makeup, report this predator, and then shoot, so instead I got to work. The burden that people place on victims of sex crimes is outrageous—was I supposed to lose my job, too?

I compartmentalized. I gave my all to Michael, to the film, to the scene. I acted, I modeled, and I performed. Then, as soon as the scene ended, I started bawling my eyes out. I couldn't believe that this had happened, and I wanted answers. Poor Michael looked terrified and confused, worried he had done something to cause my reaction. "Did I do something wrong, Tasha?" I assured him he had not—that he was not the problem. I too would have been perplexed if I just had sex with someone and they were acting the way I was acting.

I looked directly into this cameraman's eyes and said, "Why did you do that to me? Why did you grab my ass and sexually assault me? Why?"

With Stormy standing right there, he said, "It was a joke."

I felt like I was living a nightmare. This guy had openly admitted what he did, and no one cared.

Stormy then took me in a bedroom and had a talk with me. "Tasha, he's so upset—you really hurt his feelings." I couldn't believe I was being gaslit by this woman I had looked up to for so long. I explained in depth over and over again what happened and how I felt. She seemed to have empathy. She seemed to be listening. But then I realized there would be no repercussions. Nothing was going to happen to this abuser. Nothing. He got to stay on set. She just wanted to wrap this movie and not lose money by having me walk off.

Being a producer, director, actress, or PA comes with a unique set of challenges. I got that. But this behavior was obscene. Was this going to be ignored? Was Stormy going to report this to Wicked Pictures' producers? What was going to happen to rectify what had already been done? I felt like my dignity, my pride, and my sense of self-worth had been taken from me.

After calming down and finishing my cry, I got back into hair and makeup and back to work. I was beside myself, but I didn't want to cost the production money by forcing them to replace me and stalling the movie any longer. I also didn't want to lose my job. I was the lead. That's how show business works; you don't get sick days or sexual violence days. You finish what you start, and so I did. I felt humiliated and used. I felt unseen and unheard. I felt like shit. I emailed Sandra, my agent.

"Hello! So . . . yesterday on set I was sexually harassed by one of Stormy's workers. Really fucking unfortunate timing. As I was filling out paperwork, he walked behind me, grabbed my ass, and even made a sexual sound as he pressed behind me. Fucking disgusting. I called him out, and there was a witness as well, although he won't comment on what happened. I confronted Stormy and him. He set a horrible tone for my shoot. I'm not okay with this behavior, and I don't want to get lawyers involved. However, I do want to be put in touch with Wicked's HR or Steve Orenstein, the owner, to notify him. They are a huge company, and there is simply no place for this behavior in my opinion. I want to make sure he's notified and does something to correct it. Firing this employee isn't even my intention. Instead—I want them to have all their employees have sexual harassment training. They use the same guys on set, and they shoot regularly, please advise."

I wasn't looking for money. People assume that if you involve a lawyer in a sexual harassment or assault case, you are looking for money. All I wanted—deeply wanted—was for this to stop happening. For other women to be able to wake up and go to set and not fear for their safety. Was this so much to ask for?

Sandra called a meeting with Steve and his contract star jessica drake. He seemed annoyed that I had this issue with his company. "Have you never been groped on set before? What were you wearing? What do you want me to do about it?" were just some of his dehumanizing questions. At one point in my career, I had met with Steve about possibly becoming one of his contract girls. I had traveled with him to Washington to test out my people skills at a Wicked event. Ironically, Stormy had been there too. I didn't get the job, but I thought he respected me.

Now, years later, I was sitting in his office telling him I didn't feel safe at work, at his company. He was pissed. He kept saying that he could try to look into "sensitivity training," as if being groped at work by a complete stranger made me too sensitive. jessica was much more progressive. She took notes and listened to what I had to say. She is an exceptionally caring individual, and I feel blessed that the industry has her in it. She regularly does charity work and raises money for disadvantaged groups of people. Steve was unhelpful at best. He just didn't get it. I left the meeting feeling unresolved.

My father had employed a wonderful attorney for his businesses, who is, ironically, primarily focused on defending the perpetrators (people doing the crimes) of harassment claims and cases. I begged for her to take my case and to represent me in a potential lawsuit against Wicked Pictures. She obliged and called me to talk about the details of the day and what I wanted to be done about it. My vision was to have protocols put in place to protect performers on set. I wanted training videos, paperwork, and education around what was appropriate set behavior. The fact that the adult industry runs businesses without basic safety protocols being enforced and with no one holding them accountable is criminal. With the influence of the #MeToo movement, I felt more confident about standing up for myself when bad things happened. I would no longer keep quiet and pretend like everything was okay. Things were not okay, and I wanted everyone to know.

Was this the first time I had been assaulted on an adult film set, or at work, for that matter? No. But it was going to be the last. I had had enough. I had finally awoken to the toxic culture that was engulfing the industry. It was there all along, I just hadn't had the tools to speak up and do something about it. I had finally heard and seen so many actresses outside of the adult industry use their voices to take action. I had overcome the shame that was being perpetuated, attempting to silence my voice. I had hit rock bottom. I was never going to let this type of behavior slide again. *Never.*

Months rolled by, and I hadn't booked a role since the incident. I couldn't determine if there was a correlation, because work had been slow before and had always ebbed and flowed. But I couldn't help feeling like maybe directors were scared to book me. Maybe they were scared that I would report them and speak out again. They knew that they were inappropriate, and they didn't want to get called out for it. I got a call from Sandra, my agent.

"Tasha, can you shoot for Skye Blue for a *Penthouse* production? It's a tutorial type of video, a boy-girl scene with Danny Mountain." I was thrilled. I loved working with Danny, and I loved working for a female director. I thought this would be easy and fun.

As soon as I got out of hair and makeup, I noticed the production assistant looking nervous. I had been in glam for nearly two hours. "Tasha . . . I have some bad news; you're being asked to leave. The cameraman won't shoot you. He says it's a liability." I was disturbed. Without any compensation, I was being asked to leave. The cameraman who had groped me months prior was on set, and they cared more about pleasing him than letting me keep my job. This was my new world. That night Danny called me to ask if I was okay because everyone had been bad mouthing me all day at work as soon as I left. Speaking about how "crazy" and "ridiculous" I was for "fabricating" a story. My own peers claiming that I had made up the story entirely for money and attention.

The Set Up was nominated for all sorts of awards that year. I was personally nominated for Best Actress in a Comedy Release. How ironic. XBIZ Awards called to ask me if I would present an award at their show, but I declined. It felt like the whole industry was against me. From social media to movie sets, my world had been turned upside down because some asshole had assaulted me at work. On Twitter, other performers were calling me a liar, saying that I made everything up. It hurt.

"LOS ANGELES — Wicked Pictures has announced a new sexual harassment training program for all of its U.S.-based production sets.

Beginning immediately, all talent and crew, whether employed by Wicked or for a contractor that plans to sell photographs, video or other product to Wicked, will be required to take a mandatory online training program that Wicked Pictures will pay for, and also sign a code of conduct agreement to ensure the safety and comfort of both performers and crew members alike.

"Since Wicked began in 1993, we have been in the business of creating ethically produced, high-quality adult entertainment, and we owe our longevity in part to every crew member and adult performer who has helped build our brand," said Wicked Pictures' owner Steve Orenstein. "We have always cared about the safety and well-being of the performers in our movies—in fact, it's why we are still one of the few companies that are condom only."

"As times change, we strive to continue that ethos and want to further ensure that everyone on-set feels respected and comfortable performing within their own personal boundaries," Orenstein added. "While reinforcing the on-set right of bodily autonomy, our goal is clear communication and respect."

Reign made a very public accusation in early 2018 of having allegedly been "innapropriately groped and sexually harassed" by a male crew member on a November 2017 Wicked set helmed by then contract director/performer Stormy Daniels.

– Wicked Pictures press release, AVN https://avn.com/business/ articles/legal/wicked-announces-new-sexual-harassment-guide-lines-847416.html

All my advocacy work had finally paid off, a big power player in our business had recognized that on set life in the adult industry was not always professional, and they were going to try to prevent another traumatic experience from happening to additional performers. Wicked Pictures is the gold standard in adult entertainment. My hope was that this new protocol and press release would set the tone for what other companies would enforce on set going forward. This was a big deal to me on every level. I was officially an activist. I was an alchemist for change in an industry that so desperately needed it.

Coda to My *Playboy* Journey:

Hef the Hypocritical Slut-Shamer

Though *Playboy* was famous for printing photos of hot, naked women and it was many people's first masturbation material—and is widely considered the start of mainstream porn—Hef never viewed it as porn.

It's hard to say whether he was right or not. Most people have heard Justice Potter Stewart's famous nondefinition of porn: "I know it when I see it." (The full quote, in *Jacobellis v. Ohio (1964)*, is: "*I shall not today attempt further to define the kinds of material I understand to be embraced within that shorthand description ['hard-core pornography'], and perhaps I could never succeed in intelligibly doing so. But I know it when I see it, and the motion picture involved in this case is not that.*")

Despite what many people think, there is no legal definition of pornography. Through a series of landmark Supreme Court cases, the court has long attempted to define what *obscenity* is—material considered to be so far beyond the pale of "community standards" that it is not considered First Amendment–protected speech. In the modern era, the court has long held that there is pornography that is not "obscene" (however the court defines that), and which thus enjoys the protection of the First Amendment.

But there is no commonly accepted legal or cultural definition of what distinguishes pornography from nude imagery that is not pornography, beyond the entirely subjective criterion of "I know it when I see it." These days, your average streaming episode of *Game of Thrones* or *Bridgerton* shows sex as graphically as the old "X-rated" Spice Network channels of the eighties or nineties.

Most people would put any genitally explicit imagery of people having sex in the "porn" category. But when it's just photographs of nude models, it gets more complicated to draw the line between pornography and nude fine art photography. Hef always thought *Playboy* was in the "fine art nude" tradition—though of course many people disagreed with him.

However one defines porn in these soft-core edge cases, Hef was always extremely opposed to women in his magazines or social circle doing hard-core porn, or any other kind of sex work, including escorting or stripping. If he ever found you had sex on camera, stripped, escorted, or did any of the other kinds of things I had already gotten into by then or was about to get into, you'd be banned from the Mansion and cut out from his life.

The hypocrisy was dazzling. After all, one of Hef's main pursuits in life was amassing a harem of what amounted to sugar babies. All his girlfriends living with him, as well as all the women sleeping with him, were not there because he was so charming (though he was indeed charming). They were not there for his good looks, or his (Viagra-induced) virility. They were there for the modeling and economic opportunity, and in the case of his girlfriend, for the "allowance" that is the hallmark of all sugar dating relationships. Hef was one of the biggest sugar daddies of all time.

In some ways, sugar dating is sex work for people who don't want to admit they're sex workers or clients. The sugar daddies want to pretend it's a "real" relationship based on the sugar baby's supposed nonmonetary "attraction" to them—which, of course, is usually an act. And most of the sugar babies feel more comfortable sugaring because it allows them plausible deniability that they're "not an escort," which is highly stigmatized. It's also a lot safer.

For the record, I have absolutely nothing against sugar dating, either on the part of sugar daddies or sugar babies. More power to them! But I do have an objection to the hypocritical whorephobia rampant in the sugar dating world: *at least I'm not seeing prostitutes*, the clients think. And *at least I'm not a prostitute*, the sugar babies often think. Yes, you are. Nothing wrong with that (I've been one, too!), but please: stop throwing sex workers under the bus by pretending you're above it all.

Every escort I know considers sugar dating to be a form of sex work (and a usually lower-paid and more labor-intensive form, compared to regular escorting). Hef was fooling himself if he thought his girlfriends were not sex workers and he was not their client. And his girlfriends were fooling themselves if they thought the same. Furthermore, many of the *Playboy* models—including me—either had been or were actively escorting with clients on the side.

Hef had women baring it all for him and posing for *Playboy* every day, but if they did something he didn't have ownership over, he'd have them excommunicated. Today, *Playboy*'s video division is licensed to MindGeek—which owns Brazzers and PornHub— but the magazine girls were always supposed to be "pure" pageant types who looked and acted as if they worked at Disneyland.

Even though, in some ways, the *Playboy* Mansion scene was a reprieve from the slut-shaming outside its storied gates (which is why I found it so liberating at the time), in other ways it was a re-instantiation of the very slut-shaming it purported to tran- scend. Hef's world was a modern and self-contradictory version of the classic madonna-whore complex: he liked it when the girls seemed innocent but bared all *only* for him and his brand.

Hef catered to the quintessential "nice but naughty" girl-next- door fantasy: "I can get off . . . but with a girl who has eyes only for me. Not with (heaven forbid!) a *slut* or a *whore*!" Once I'd decided to go outside of that fantasy of innocence into porn— which forever marked me, in society's eyes, as a slut and whore—I knew there wouldn't be a place for me at the Mansion anymore.

While I was on the *Playboy* scene, I successfully hid that I'd been an escort and a stripper before. It's much harder to hide that you're a porn star when your face (and much more) is plastered on screens and DVD covers across the land. Looking back, I resent the degree to which Hef controlled us with his "innocent girl" fantasy. I couldn't say who I was, where I'd been, or what I dreamed of (being the next Jenna Jameson). We were supposed to be extremely sexy . . . but no, not in *that* way! In the "good girl" kind of way (whatever that is).

It was enough to drive a woman crazy, trying to find just the right amount of overt sexuality to please Hef, but not too much. It's complicated—I truly enjoyed my time there. But looking back, I can say that worrying so much about what a man thinks of me, and trying to fit in his box of the "right" amount of sexy to not seem like a "slut," doesn't align with my feminist ideals of today. I don't ever want to feel again like I have to be a certain type of person or look a certain way in order to be accepted.

Of course, no matter who you are or what you do, some people are always going to judge you. That's a reality of life. But I never want to put pressure on myself to exist in a way that doesn't involve living my truth. I suppressed my truth while at the Mansion for years—the truth that I wanted to be a famous porn star. I suppressed it because being accepted by Hef and by the scenesters there made me feel powerful. But what power did I really have? None, if Hef said so. And eventually, he said so.

When Hef found out I was going to do porn, he told me I couldn't come to Movie Night or Fun in the Sun anymore, and that I couldn't pose for *Playboy*. I wasn't welcome back at the Mansion, ever. I still have the letter he wrote me about it to this day.

I knew he'd say those things, and I thought his arbitrary rules were crazy, but still, it hurt. I had thought we were friends. His judgmental letter showed just how deep this "friendship" really was. At the same time, it gave me closure. It allowed me to focus on my career and do what I wanted.

And what I wanted to do was become one of the biggest porn stars in the land. And I was well on my way.

But as you've seen, there was one more man in the industry I gave all my power away to, right after Hef: Devon, boyfriend, agent, and pseudo-pimp.

Now it was time to break free.

Inequality and
Advocacy Work

Race, gender, education, attractiveness, accolades, and experience all play a role in determining privilege in the adult industry. The fact I am a white woman, with a higher education, heteronormatively beautiful, and have invested a ton of money and time in the business are all reasons why I have had privilege in porn. I speak solely for myself when I speak of my experience in the adult business. When it comes to race, I have witnessed the way white directors treat Black performers and even how Black directors treat Black performers. I've been on numerous sets with Black talent where the director treated the man or woman with disrespect and used racist commentary. The most challenging part of this predicament is that as a performer, you don't want to be the reason that the other performer doesn't get paid that day. There are also only so many times I could have kept harping on about how unethical on-set life was before no one wanted to hire me again, which ultimately ended up happening. These are a few of those moments.

The adult industry is racist. I deeply believe that art reflects life and that pornography is not an exception. When I got into the print side of the adult industry in 2010, I didn't think much of the fact that people of color weren't photographed in the magazines I appeared in. Not on purpose—I just didn't think much of it. That is strange in retrospect, as I was a women's studies major who specifically studied race, gender, and intersectionality. I was in denial, because why would I want to associate with an industry that was racist? Well, the tough truth is that entertainment in general is, and I think that goes back to art reflecting life. America is racist.

My agent would say openly that doing "IR," interracial scenes, would lower my worth in the marketplace. *Interracial* is a word for performing specifically with Black talent, not any other person of color. If you are a white woman and you have sex with an Asian man or a Mexican man, this is not IR, but if the person is Black, or looks Black, then that is IR. What in the actual fuck, right? But what did lowering my worth mean? Simply put, that if I chose to do IR, then other people wouldn't want to use me in their movies, my financial value as a commodity would drop, I wouldn't be able to charge my rate, and lastly my brand would somehow be diminished.

Before going any further, I want to note that at the time I started adult work, all the IR companies that I had heard of, even mainstream IR focused companies, were truly horrendous. I wouldn't have worked for these producers anyway. They were low-budget, blatantly racist, and not popular. Nothing would have drawn me to shooting for a director who was going to perpetuate some discriminatory stereotype or make the male performer look bad, in turn reflecting on me. So I just stayed away. I thought, why would I want to shoot something controversial? Fast-forward to my work in the Sunshine State.

Florida is a place where you don't want to be performing in adult film. Full of seedy people and a more sexist on-set culture, Florida has always been a last resort place to film for me. If you're a woman who's spent most of your career performing in the San Fernando Valley, only to be thrown into the Miami scene, you will be terribly disappointed. The main company that thrives there, Bang Bros, uses pressure tactics, which feel coercive to me, and I have heard horror stories about them. On this project, I was adamant about wanting to see the male talent before the shoot dates. Even though they were amateur, I thought it was reasonable to know whom I was going to be performing with. Everyone had to get a start somewhere, right? I hadn't ever been in a sex scene until I had. Why would this be any different? These men wanted to try to see if they had what it takes to be performers.

I should have watched the videos on this site beforehand. Always watch the videos. Even my agent warned me against going. But I needed the money and the relevancy. These were mostly random men and women who were offered money to be in adult movies. They were tested, of course, but potentially had no intention of joining the industry before being asked to. It drew an unfamiliar crowd, with an overall attitude that I was not used to. This was not Los Angeles talent. The company agreed to inform me of the talent prior to shooting so I could approve of them. When it came time to shoot with the first-timers, the company scrambled to get confirmations that they were tested negative for STD's and ready to shoot, so I only got to see photos of the talent last minute. I don't know what the back-end issue was, but I was told the same day I was going to be shooting with a man who in his photo looked . . . Black. Up until this time I had been told over and over again by my agent that I was not to do IR. And now, without my consent, I was being thrust into an IR scene?

"Devon! Devon! Did you know I was shooting IR today?" I shouted into my cell phone.

"Tasha, calm down. You're not shooting IR. I will have Bang Bros send over a photo of the performer now." And just like that, I felt gaslit. Why was I being told that this man was not Black when in fact he was? My whole career, I was brainwashed to believe that if a man's skin was "too dark," then I would be less valuable as an artist. In the end, it turned out that this guy was simply a Latino man who happened to get a summer tan before our shoot. I was floored. Why didn't it matter that his skin was just as dark as a light-skinned Black man? Why was there such a huge difference between being Black and being a dark-skinned Latino man? In the end I shot my scene. It was a turbulent experience because of the asshole director that day. It was one of my worst days on set—and one of my fans' favorite scenes, go figure.

The business would soon change the way it shot IR porn, starting with a company called Blacked, but it would take years. Although the Black-and-white fetish is still very popular, now there are plenty of websites that shoot this genre in an elegant manner, similar to the way non-IR films are shot. Depending on one's perspective, any IR could seem racist, but as an insider who has shot the genre, I would say that people of all color enjoy the niche, and to make it more normalized and less derogatory is certainly a step in the right direction.

In 2017, I went on a two-month-long vacation to explore Europe. I had a text from Greg Lansky inquiring about shooting me for his new production company, Blacked. Greg was an extremely talented director. He knew what high-end art looked like, and he knew how to make it. Greg and I had a rough shoot in the very beginning of my career. It was one of my first girl-girl shoots ever, and I didn't really understand what to do. I had kissed a girl before but never given or received oral sex from one. I also was assigned to work with some strong female performers who were nothing short of expert, so I just did what I knew how to do—posed for photos and faked it. Greg ended up telling my agent that I shouldn't be on set and how awful my performance was, knowing damn well Devon would make me cry about it. He also wrote a nasty little blog post about just how bad my performance was. I was stunned. He hadn't hired me since, so I was utterly shocked when he wanted to hire me again seven years later.

Greg told me about his plan to put me in a scene for his new company and how impactful it would be. I was thrilled. I immediately told Devon about the proposal. "Devon! Greg has a new company that he wants to shoot me for . . . Blacked! He says it's artful and beautiful and will be a huge hit."

Devon, not surprisingly, responded with dismay. "No, you are not doing interracial porn. It will lower your value in the workplace, Tasha." Devon always had the final word when it came to my shoots, so I had to respectfully decline. Devon's old-fashioned thinking would not dictate my future, but it certainly controlled what I did and didn't do at this time in my life. I would like to mention that female talent is often paid more to work with Black male talent.

Devon and I kept butting heads, and we kept arguing. I was no longer a go-with-the-flow woman—quite the opposite.

"I think you've outgrown the industry, Tasha," Devon said in his stern English accent.

"But Devon, this man jumped on stage with me, in the middle of my set at Sapphires gentlemen's club. I just want to be protected at work," I said defensively.

"Well, I heard you were pulling customers on stage, so he must have thought he could." Slut-shame. Slut-shame. Slut-shame. It was all I could hear. "I also heard that you're telling customers they can't touch you before going into private rooms for lap dances after the show." Silence. This conversation was going nowhere.

"Yes, I do tell them that, because I don't want to be harassed and assaulted," I said as passionately as I could. Devon didn't want me as a model anymore, it was clear. I wasn't making the kind of money I used to for him, so he needn't pretend like he cared about my well-being anymore. He didn't need me. If anything, my constant complaints about not being safe at work were a nuisance to him. He didn't want to be held accountable for what he considered nonsense, and he was letting me go. Our relationship of seven years was ending because he was sick of the truth. The truth was expensive, and I was willing to pay.

"Goodbye, Devon. You're right, I have outgrown the business." And that was that—no more Devon. It was as if he had fallen off the face of the Earth, or maybe I had. Either way, it was a bittersweet ending to a dysfunctional relationship. I notified a few companies I had been wanting to work with that I had left his agency. I was booked immediately.

Racism in the adult industry is still prominent. People of color would be able to speak more articulately about the topic than I can. From my perspective, it seems as though the new generation of performers, even elder millennials, are trying their best to dismantle racism on set and through the adult industry by casting more Black performers in roles that do not other them for their color. The older producers and directors are still stuck in the eighties, but their opinions and thoughts matter less with each minute that passes. More and more I see inclusive websites, movies, and overall content that speak to our generation. Some of the biggest sites in XXX focus on glamorizing Black men. Not everyone will think that is necessarily less racist, but I do. Porn imitates societal values.

My obsession with crime stories surrounding sex workers rose from becoming a sex worker myself. There is no other way to put this: once I became one, the fear of being raped or killed and targeted because of my job kicked in. Which is a crazy concept to think about. I have a glorified, often celebrated occupation, with millions of fans. I make hundreds of thousands of dollars a year. I enjoy my occupation, and it's legal. Yet, somehow it is simultaneously a career choice that makes the American legal system, law enforcement, and society as a whole believe that you are rapeable. Because of the senseless crimes among sex workers that occur with absolutely no justice, the fear grows daily. I am drawn to television shows that feature true crime stories about sex workers. I listen to daily podcasts, watch documentaries, and can't get enough of these real-life stories. Psychologically, it is because I so badly want the release of watching the content and being able to say, "Phew! At least it wasn't me!"

It's a release and closure. I am empathetic about the stories, but I am still relieved that it's not me that has to endure it—at least not today. I have privilege both in the type of sex work I engage in currently and in my socioeconomic status, but I am still aware of the way we are treated when it comes to crime. Slut-shaming and victim blaming have not subsided, and when something happens to one of us, the familiar response is "She was asking for it!" Maybe it's the firsthand experiences that have led me to this conclusion or that the media blares the message loud and clear every time it addresses the subject, but it's heartbreaking. I hope that with advocacy work, education, and more political candidates who care about sex workers, the laws and the media treatment will change for us. I have this wish for our future generations, for myself, and for society as a whole. No one should have their human rights taken away because of their chosen career path. Therefore, I decided to run for chairperson of the Adult Performer Advocacy Committee.

I soon found out that I was alone in my mission to make performing safer regarding sexual harassment and assault on set. I was devastated. Every time I spoke up, the other council members seemed to have different interests. I don't think anyone joins the adult business, specifically porn, and thinks, *Today I may lose my rights to my most basic protections for the rest of my life for a small paycheck* . . . but that's exactly what happens when you choose to wear the scarlet letter of the adult industry. People try to warn you. The first time I ever stepped foot on an adult film set, it was for Digital Playground. The male talent, whom I was a fan of at the time, asked me if I wanted to go to dinner. He was working with a beautiful new contract star, Selena Rose, that day.

After I heard and watched a little of their loud sex scene from a corner, he approached me. I was flattered and enthusiastically agreed to the date. We went to Geisha House, a fancy sushi restaurant, and I was enamored. "Rachel, I wouldn't do this. Do not join this business. I feel like it is my duty to stop new women from ruining their lives," he said with complete seriousness. "My ex-wife has people tagging her storefront in Orange County with the words *Whore* and *Slut* in red ink. You will not be able to live the life you are used to. But for me, as a man, it's different." I wasn't disenchanted by what he was saying, but I was interested in trying to date him. So I took his advice for a couple of weeks and put off my urge to go down to the testing facility at the time and join the business. His director on set that day, Robby D, had asked me to do so. Scott, the performer, ended up being a player. So after I realized my dream man wasn't going to be my boyfriend, I threw his warning out the window.

Friends asked, "What are you going to do after porn?" They implied that if I joined the business, there would be nothing for me afterward. No hope, no future, as if it was some sort of death sentence. But for me, when I was determined to join the business (and I know I am not alone), there was absolutely no changing my mind. No one, not even a famous porn star, could deter me from having sex on camera. My stubborn twenty-one-year-old mind was made up. I live my life without regret but take lessons from every chapter, so I hope you can read mine and at least become aware of the dark details I was unaware of.

Disownment was one consequence. Before deciding to have sex on film, one must realize that the act in and of itself is extremely controversial. Therefore, some if not all members of your immediate and distant family may disown you. I couldn't dodge judgement from everyone under the sun. My stepmother cut me off as soon as my father died, claiming that the insurance money I got was enough to cover all my costs of living. Meanwhile, she lied to my dad on his deathbed and told him that she would take care of me forever, throw me my wedding, maintain the lifestyle I had been accustomed to. After my father's death, her sister, my dear aunt Annie, our family financial adviser, reached out to me via email. Darcy did as well—right after filing a police report against me. Darcy claimed I had stolen my father's jewelry from his home; I had been in Los Angeles at the time. Incidents like this were nothing new when it came to Darcy. They both claimed that if I was enrolled as a full-time student, they would cover my necessary expenses. But knowing that Darcy and her three children were living luxuriously off my father's money made me sick. I wanted nothing to do with these wannabes. Their father was and is alive and well; mine was dead.

I had officially been cut off. My stepmother called me a whore and slut, throwing my artistic nudes at me as she kicked me out of the house the day my father died. She sent my mother hateful emails of me fucking men on film, with links to my most outrageous porn videos. My little sister stopped talking to me all together, and one of my older sisters claimed she needed therapy from trauma she had suffered watching me "turn to porn." It was a never-ending parade of friends and family members who no longer wanted to be associated with me. It hurt badly. But that was just the beginning of the unfortunate disapproval of society for a seemingly legal career. I was stumped and confused how anyone's reaction to my profession could be this dramatic.

The shame that society throws at you is challenging to summarize. I have been fortunate to avoid, through luck, privilege, and disinterest, any of the harrowing challenges that will inevitably affect many performers as they choose to have sex on film. Performers and workers in the industry (managers, makeup artists, camera guys) throughout my career have spoken up about having their entire bank accounts shut down overnight with no warning whatsoever. Many performers who have gone on to other careers, even medical professionals, have been fired for having worked on OnlyFans. Discriminating against people for making a living legally shouldn't be tolerated, but it somehow is.

One of the most riveting interviews I've watched was with Bree Olson, who is known outside the industry for being Charlie Sheen's girlfriend. She told the world what her personal experience has been as an adult film star functioning in the real world. At one point in the interview, she breaks down sobbing about how the treatment parallels being looked at like a pedophile. I've never heard of anything more apropos. It's a disgusting way to think about myself, so I had never said the words aloud. But then, when Bree said them, it hit me: "Society has been treating me like I would be dangerous to children. Why?" My own sister wouldn't let me around her children because she viewed me as a bad role model. Apparently, schools won't let me teach youth. Women in porn are constantly getting their own children taken away from them in court after a divorce, claiming they are unfit mothers. I often worry about these topics. What if my future partner tried to do this? Who would protect me?

"That's my daughter," my mother exclaimed to our server. She was looking at the cover of OC Weekly, Orange County's weekly newspaper. I had scored a front-page cover of one of our county's most coveted publications. Wearing pigtails, a miniskirt, and a matching top, I had a schoolgirl-themed aura. I looked cute and young and successful. Never had an adult actress graced our conservative county's newspaper, but I was there making history and making my mom proud. All a daughter wants to do is to make her family proud.

"I feel ashamed to show my face at the local grocery store, to make eye contact with the cashier," she would say to me, in reference to my career in adult. Her shame and projected fears wore on me, but as much as I wanted to make her proud, I couldn't live my life for someone else. It broke my heart that my mom and some family members only accepted the work I chose to do and take pride in after I reached a mainstream platform. It was as if they were saying, "Until the rest of society accepts you, then we can't support your craft or choices." What if I hadn't been able to gain mainstream acceptance or even success? Would they still be treating me like a second-class citizen?

The Evolution of OnlyFans

OnlyFans emerged on the scene in 2016 and slowly but surely changed the trajectory of the adult business. Historically, we as performers have had the option of owning our websites where we could shoot content, interact with fans, and be in charge. It had been a passive side income for me, but certainly not my bread and butter. It was more of a creative outlet for my quality content, partially because it was fun and partially because it was entrepreneurial. Picking out the theme, hiring the talent, choosing makeup, finding wardrobe, directing, performing—it's a lot of work. My favorite film that I directed was called *Tasha's Pony Tales*. From bedazzling the lingerie with rhinestones to creating beautifully blown glass dildos, I was involved in every part of the movie. The overhead costs were high to achieve what I wanted as a director and as an artist, so it was not the most lucrative way to make income, although it was enjoyable because I was in control.

When OnlyFans broke out on the scene, my interest was piqued. It was a way to cut costs by appealing to the amateur fans. No overhead would be needed, and the style was easy to produce. Snapping selfies in a bathroom or simply chatting live on the app was appealing to me, as it was to many others. It seemed like there would be a lot of money in it, and more importantly to me, it was safe. Safe from the control of men on set. Safe from creepy agents and producers, and safe from directors abusing their power. Cutting out the middleman entirely, OnlyFans defined a new chapter in porn.

To set up your profile, you simply upload a profile photo, a description of yourself and your page, fill out some admin paperwork, and it's go time! You can upload as much or as little content as you want to. You can go as soft or as hard-core as you would like, and there are a ton of built-in options for interaction, such as live shows and campaigns, but ultimately it is a pretty simple setup. The key to success on OnlyFans is to get creative with content and drive traffic to your site through social media. Most social media platforms are not adult-friendly, so it's imperative to find loopholes to promote your brand, whether that be through code words or sneaky Instagram handles. It's a tricky terrain. I once paid someone thousands of dollars to get my Instagram handle back because it was taken away for inappropriate content, which is subjective. You can shoot from home, on vacation, or even your own set; whatever your vision is, there are people willing and wanting to consume it. Be careful about where on vacation you choose to shoot, though, because people have been arrested and even held in jails due to content creation overseas!

As word spread, people who weren't even doing adult were using the platform. It seemed like that was a boundary that needed to be crossed in order to make porn more acceptable. OnlyFans soon was a mainstream site used by all sorts of entertainers, from athletes to musicians. My dream had come true; adult content had finally been normalized, at least among my generation. It is now a genre of film that is just another form of entertainment, not necessarily controversial to the masses. OnlyFans is a way for entertainers to connect with their fans and to monetize that connection through the internet. My interest slowly but surely went into the direction of creating my own content as my main income from porn. It was great timing, because my career on mainstream adult film sets had hit a lull, and the bookings were few and far between. I was in the midst of the #MeToo movement, and I wasn't really being hired to come on sets for bigger-name companies. It was a mind fuck, because I couldn't figure out if I was being blacklisted because I was speaking out against the predators in the industry or if it was me getting older and gaining weight, therefore depreciating my value in the marketplace. Maybe it was a mix of both, but I could still remain in adult with OnlyFans.

OnlyFans is the answer to so many performers' issues. Whether or not it's what the founders intended, it has made shooting porn safer. If I'm not at the whim of a director—instead I am the one calling all the shots—then I am safer. If I don't have to be around seedy cameramen and questionable people, then I am safer. It takes out a lot of the problematic issues on set and gives the performer creative control. When new women ask me how to get into the adult business, I always suggest getting onto a camming site first to grow a brand and an audience. That is a place where you appear virtually for tons of fans on one website from the comfort of wherever it is you are. That way the model can get comfortable in front of the camera and also get people hyped about their online presence. Create social media platforms so that people can follow what you're up to and what you are doing. Then they can engage with your online persona. You can be a completely fictional character or somebody more similar to your true self—the choice is yours! Then comes the fun part: shooting content that appeals to you.

It is my belief that what you enjoy shooting, your fans will enjoy watching. There is no need to push yourself to do acts that you don't want to do. You can absolutely just model in a bikini if that is your limit, or go further and bring in another performer; the content just needs to be fun and consensual.

Becoming an Heiress

In the summer of 2017, I got a text from my older half sister, my father's daughter from his first marriage. She is a divorce attorney with three children, and I'm close with her. Miranda is there for me when I need her most, and at fifteen years my senior, she acts as a surrogate parent to me. "Darcy has died," she notified me. It was painful news. Darcy was a tortured human. But aren't we all? Some of us just showcase our trauma more flamboyantly, and she was one of those people.

I was immediately asked not to attend the funeral by my estranged stepsiblings, through a family member. The tension that followed my father's death was extreme. But extreme enough to be barred from my own stepmother's funeral? I think not. Annie, my financial adviser and stepaunt (Darcy's sister), invited my older sister and me down to her office to discuss finances. Walking into Morgan Stanley, I had no idea we had any money left in our trust fund. I assumed Darcy had drained our accounts and what was done was done; after all, she was a drug addict and a big spender. As Miranda and I walked through the bank's doors in Beverly Hills, I had no idea my life was about to change forever.

Annie was waiting for us in her office. I hadn't spoken with her since my father had died and she had cut me off. She was eager to get us to sign away the $8 million home my father left behind, thinking she would have included us in the profits. Darcy did not. "Your trust funds have millions of dollars in them, including all of these real-estate developments and assets: stocks, bonds, restaurants, retirement communities . . . it's all yours now." My sister and I were shocked. We quickly signed the paperwork. I went to bed one night a self-made adult performer, and I woke up an heiress to millions of dollars. I did not fully realize that it would change my circumstances so drastically.

Now I could relax. I could focus on dating and creating a family. I could stop traveling for feature dancing and worrying about work. I had finally received what was mine, what my father had built for me, and I couldn't be more grateful. It's one thing to come from wealth and inherit a trust fund. It is quite another to come from wealth, have it completely stripped away at twenty years old, never thinking I'd get it back, then to wake up nearly ten years later and become a multimillionaire overnight. I felt great gratitude in every part of my being.

Money is great but money can also be dark. You never know if people want to date you for your money. If friends want to be your friends because you have money. And there will always be someone that has more money than you. That's the inconvenient part about having money.

Falling
in Love

The expectations that my partners have had for my bedroom performance and desires have not always matched up to reality, due to my alter ego as Tasha Reign. I like sex as much as the next woman, in my twenties even more than I do now in my thirties. I hear your forties is where you have "the best sex of your life!" I am also great at performance, and if I really want to put on a show . . . I can. But it is not my current passion. I do not live and breathe sex. Often, I would prefer to watch a movie or go shopping, maybe eat a delicious meal. The sad truth is that my partners always feel let down when it comes to my sex drive, knowing what a strong performer I am. I wish it wasn't the case.

On the other hand, I have become a size queen. Sure, I can deal with an average-sized dick, but I would prefer a porn-sized cock. In both of my most recent relationships, the topic of me not liking sex has been brought up by my partners. The thing about sex is that it happens outside of the bedroom as well, in the foreplay, the buildup. I am not a machine who can be turned on and turned off at the press of a button. I want the buildup to the moment to take thought. I need to be courted. It's psychological for me; otherwise, I should be getting paid.

Swipe left, swipe right, swipe all night; that's how the mantra goes. I was so over dating apps and ready to find my person. I turned thirty and had what felt like a midlife crisis. How did this much time pass? Where did my life go? Why wasn't I married with children? Were my twenties really over? I wasn't settling into adulthood very smoothly; in fact, I wasn't embracing my age at all. I was dreading it. I felt like time had passed by me and that I was never going to meet anyone.

And then I met him, at Shutters, a hotel in Santa Monica, upstairs in the penthouse restaurant overlooking the city. All the furniture and decor are white, and it feels clean and modern, a perfect setting to start a new chapter. He was tall, blond, had a half sleeve of unique tattoos, and he was oh so handsome. I do have a type. The conversation was light and the food delicious. Kelen was confident, sweet, and had a boyish smile that made me swoon. I loved that he didn't pry into my adult career. In fact, he never brought it up, which made me like him even more than I already did. He knew very well what I did for work.

My job has always been a touchy subject. I've never felt comfortable discussing it with a stranger at dinner; the questions they often ask are inappropriate. It's not even the person's fault, but the actual subject matter is literally inappropriate dinner conversation for someone you just met. Being too complimentary surrounding the topic invokes a type of fan vibe that is a real turn-off; I didn't want to date a fan. Being antisex work about my career would never work, either; that would have immediately turned me off as well. The best route was to do exactly what he did: just ignore the subject at hand. I often wish that my job was not such a polarizing and controversial topic for new people to understand, that men and women could just see me the way they see a schoolteacher or a housewife. To be seen through the lens of whore for over a decade does something to the soul. "Don't let the world harden you," my coworker Lexi Belle once said to me at a convention; not thinking much of it, I just shrugged my shoulders. Years later it really sank in: how could someone be treated the way sex workers are treated in our patriarchal, slut-shaming society and not let the world harden them?

I had been on so many dates that had seemingly gone "really well," only to be ghosted or find out that they didn't want what I had been up front about looking for: a long-term, committed relationship. I was transparent in my dating app profiles: "Seeking love, must want children! Looking for a genuine connection." I never wanted anyone to be confused or surprised about my intentions for dating. I was happy that after our comfortable first date, Kelen continued to text. I was even more ecstatic when he asked me to be his valentine. I hadn't had a real love connection on Valentine's Day since before I could remember, maybe since high school.

Holidays are extremely important to me. In my adulthood, they have often been celebrated in fun costumes for work or parties. I've always thought sanctifying moments and throwing themed parties was my calling, but with no one romantic to share them with, they felt empty. It was clear he had put so much thought and effort into our special night, with gifts, a beach visit, and fancy dinner reservations. I was falling fast. I had held out for sex until that special night, when I knew we were official. I had him hooked, and he had my heart. Our honeymoon period was passionate, and I felt like I had found my husband. Time flew. We loved spending time doing nothing but eating yummy food, watching crime documentaries, playing with our dogs, and fucking. We fucked a lot. I loved sex with him. I trained him to eat me out, and I gave him the best head he ever had, or at least that's what he told me. I mean . . . I had been nominated for best oral sex by the XBIZ Awards, so I wasn't surprised.

Life was good and easy. My new trust fund situation was tempting. I could take us on decadent trips. He would contribute as much as he could, and I covered the rest. I wasn't resentful at first; I was just happy to be with this sweet and handsome guy who seemed to accept me for me. I was still performing with men for my OnlyFans.

"It's just my brand and just my job, nothing else," I tried to explain to him.

"I can smell him on you," he would say, referring to the male talent, as he tried to persuade me to stop doing boy-girl scenes. He gave me the ultimatum that most civilians—men outside of porn—give us female performers: "You can either choose me, or you can perform with guys, but I'm not okay with you performing with dudes and being with me." This chat was usually inevitable, something to be expected from our male counterparts. But of course when the shoe is on the other foot, that conversation looks different. It is my personal experience that women tend to be more understanding when it comes to sex work.

I took the leap of faith and agreed to stop performing with male performers. Cock was important, but my love life and future were far more important. When you turn thirty in LA, something in your brain switches, as if a higher power whispers in your ear, "Tick-tock, time's running out." Or at least this is how I felt. Kelen was a catch. He came from a wealthy family, I was extremely attracted to him, and he claimed to want to build a family like I did, so I was all in. We lived in a big house in the Hollywood Hills, with two French bulldogs, two Chihuahuas, and a couple of fabulous cars. I was head over heels in love with this man. He was tall, blond, and handsome, but most of all he was young, fun, and treated me like a normal girl. I didn't feel othered by him. I felt like he saw me for me. I wanted to impress Kelen, I wanted to show him the life we could live, and I most of all I wanted a future with him.

Kelen's main downside was that he was sober. Which meant his first priority was always himself. Addicts can be fun, but the fact he was so obsessed with the identity of being sober was something I could never accept. He loved his AA group, and most of all his mentor and sponsor, Jim F. He placed him on a pedestal far above me, and that was clear from the start. He loved that Jim was a celebrity, and he always reminded me that I wasn't on the same playing field as him. It was not only offensive but weird, as if he wanted to put me in my place. I was rarely included in social activities, but when I was, Kelen wouldn't want to show affection, and he seemed to really care how I looked. It didn't help the situation that his sober friends were rarely married or fathers themselves, so it's not like his LA friends had a trajectory that I wanted him to follow. I always felt second to Jim and his cronies.

After a year, when he agreed to move in with me, we went house hunting. He didn't like my cottage in the woods of Topanga Canyon; he didn't think it was big enough, nice enough, or close enough to his work. I would choose less expensive homes, and he would show me houses that cost twice as much. He felt entitled, because I had recently had a rental house that I had told him about, and he wanted to match that price point. Sure, he would be chipping in, but not by half—more like a third. His parents funded his life, and I wanted nothing more than to please him. He had it made in the shade. We moved into a modern home on Caverna Drive.

My baby fever quickly kicked in after we moved in together. I hadn't grown up in a home with a healthy, positive marriage, although I always thought of myself as someone who would have that one day. I didn't feel like a ring or license would somehow make us more official than we already were, and I wanted a baby. That was my most primal desire. In my heart, in my veins, in my soul, all I wanted was to be a mom. I knew at six months into our relationship that I wanted a baby with him, so how much longer did I have to wait?

Apparently, a while longer. He needed time. He wanted to be married first, and he wanted another year at least. I prayed and hoped and wished that I could commit to this and keep my timeline flexible. The truth is women are raised to be patient, to be humble—to be doormats.

I wanted to call the shots. I wanted to create my destiny on my timeline. Kelen started to get more and more comfortable with the idea of marriage, so we went ring shopping. He didn't offer to contribute, because he wasn't financially in a place to do so, but opening an account where he could deposit a few bucks each month seemed like a decent alternative.

"No, I'll be paying that off for the rest of my life!" he exclaimed when I brought up the idea. This wasn't the romantic picture I had in my mind of marriage, and my expectations weren't meeting up with reality. I was resentful. Everything had changed since we'd moved in together. The financial and emotional inequality in the relationship was too stark to bear. Don't get me wrong—Kelen (with his parents' money) contributed to our lives, but it was clear he was not ready for what I wanted. He also had expensive tastes; when we were looking at homes to buy, he wanted the pricier ones. When I offered to pay for dinner, he wanted me to order the best. He constantly commented on my lack of fashion and would even make me change before going out with his friends. Sure, his best friend was James Franco, but how superficial can you be? I had cute clothing and great taste. He would blast our overpriced air-conditioning. LA is so expensive! He would food shame me about eating "badly." Los Angeles seems to create men who are obsessed with health, weight, looks, and of course their girlfriend's "health" as well. I couldn't believe he had the audacity to call me out when I wanted to order a veggie burger. Or look at me with disgust when I would treat myself to carbs.

"If you ever gain as much weight as your sister, I'm leaving!"

he stated matter-of-factly one day as I stood up for weight fluc-tuation in relationships. Yes, I had gained a few extra pounds in 2020—who the fuck hadn't? He had shed the pounds and wanted me to as well. He said he was trying to keep me accountable, but it got the point where I had to hide my food in our TV room because of his supposed "food addiction." He was addicted to everything except sex.

But he shot some great porn. Truly, some of my favorite Only-Fans content and "amateur pictures" were shot by him. He was creative. He fucked me well and had a nice dick. He loved dogs. He was playful. My friends liked him. Those were the positives.

Money quickly became our most troubling issue: who had it, and who didn't. A trust fund may seem like an advantage, and it was, but it really fucked with my head. It was as if the financial struggles I had been through just never happened, and now I could afford to live well beyond what I had been accustomed to. Life was easier when I didn't have to think about how much money I had in stocks and how much I was spending on luxury travel, when I was restricted to coming up with the funds to pay basic bills and sometimes scrape by. Who am I kidding? I was often scraping by because work was never promised and budgeting wasn't some-thing I was raised to do. But the only person before Kelen to be unforgiving of me was myself. Now, because the power dynamic of our relationship was about money, I felt like I was giving every-thing, and he was giving less than half. Moving in with Kelen changed the dynamic of what we had, and not in a good way. December came, and I wasn't happy because I didn't feel like we were headed toward marriage. January came, and I grew more and more resentful. February came, and he agreed to go wedding-ring shopping.

For his birthday, I booked us an over-the-water bungalow at the Four Seasons, Bora Bora, because I was still overspending my trust fund money and still trying to persuade Kelen to see me as the mother of his children. I also wanted to shoot OnlyFans content. He obliged. By Valentine's Day, when I realized his motivation to get an engagement ring seemed almost nonexistent, I felt furious. I felt like I was dragging him into a life he wasn't interested in.

"Sometimes I feel like this is your life and I'm just along for the ride," he said to me one night. It hurt knowing that the man that I loved so deeply wasn't on the same page as me, and my love quickly turned into hate. Anything he did would tick me off, and I mean anything. He forgot to order me the vegetarian option on our fifteen-hour plane ride to Malaysia, and my fury knew no bounds. I didn't feel safe with him or trust him to stand up for me; when we got to the resort and a fellow tourist got too close to me while clearly wasted and ranting, I was immediately upset that Kelen wasn't "protecting" me. My trauma of sexual assault and harassment from my past hadn't been properly processed, and thus I dumped my fear and anger onto Kelen throughout the trip. But we did manage to have sex—for OnlyFans, and because he wouldn't stop stroking his cock with Bora Bora's locally sourced oil. With large glass windows surrounding us in this gorgeous hut in the middle of the ocean, anyone would have been turned on.

As we went at it, Kelen requested my least favorite position, reverse cowgirl. It is my belief that it's not a real sex position but one that the porn world made up for show. It's so much work to do, and I personally don't care for it. "What's wrong with you? It's like you're broken!" he said, referring to my distaste for reverse cowgirl, as if I was a wind-up doll that couldn't perform his favorite act. I was disgusted by his attitude, but I just wanted to please him, so I continued the act until he finished.

The last straw was when I booked us to go on a snorkeling trip with about ten other people. We had our own tour guide who was taking us to snorkel with lemon sharks, which are pretty safe to swim with, but sharks nonetheless. Kelen and I had been butting heads in paradise. The clear blue waters, the tropical fish, the long kayaks and island food would have been my dream if I wasn't so miserable. I couldn't hush my inner voice: *You want a baby. He's not going to give you a baby now!*

As we took off into the crystal-clear waters, I wore a one-piece black bathing suit that showed my cleavage, because I have triple-D breasts and everything shows my cleavage. I was the only woman on this little boat, other than one other lady, who was fully covered. The boat captain began his little speech about the ocean and the sharks and then looked me directly in the eye and said, "Keep your titties covered, because the sharks will bite your titties!" The whole boat chuckled at his misogynistic joke, including Kelen. I was floored. I felt as though it was a personal attack, and it hurt. I asked Kelen if he had heard what this creep said. He responded as if he actually didn't hear, or as if my question wasn't valid. And that was truly it: validation. Kelen never seemed to validate my thoughts, dreams, or desires. Our entire relationship was invalidating. In that moment, I yearned for a man to stand up for me, to say something to our boat captain, to tell me he would report him, anything. Instead, Kelen snarled at me and hopped in the water to chat with the captain about the fish, and the rest of the trip was ruined.

By the time we got back to the States, we wanted to work out our difficulties in therapy. My underlying issue was wanting him to be passionate about having children, but that's a desire you can't force on anyone. "Men are not as openly excited to have children until the child is born," our therapist said to me when I brought it up over and over again. For someone who values consent, I was pushing myself on him. I thought the more I spoke about it the more he would gain familiarity and want to have kids as well. He ended up committing to a month to start trying for babies and I was relieved. Finally, we had something on the calendar.

I wanted to salvage our relationship. My first threesome with Kelen sums up our two years of time together. There was a lack of communication and a lack of emotional availability throughout. I'm not placing all the blame on him; I should have known better with all those years on set. I did not foresee how different the threesome experience would be with a real-life boyfriend. Also, I didn't realize how imperative it would be to communicate about expectations and wants to him.

"It would be fun to shoot a threesome for my OnlyFans, babe," I would say to him from time to time. Finally, I found a really cute brunette from Australia whom he was down to shoot with. We were filming our very first threesome on camera, which was personal to me. It was POV (point-of-view shooting, meaning Kelen was also the camera guy) and the only real reason he was doing it was for the sexual experience. I thought it would bring us closer together. I booked the gig through Twitter DM, and it was on. In a very casual way we drove to downtown Los Angeles and walked up to Charlette's suite, as if we had done this before. Kelen nonchalantly filled out the paperwork and then strapped on his POV headband with a camera attached to it. We didn't speak about checking in with one another or making me feel like I was his girlfriend during sex—we just had shitty sex, and then boom, the scene was over. When I looked at him with a distressed expression afterward, he dismissed it immediately.

"Oh, come on don't look at me like that," he said, as if there was no room for discussion. And that was that. I couldn't speak my mind, and my emotions were pushed away once again. I felt like he didn't pay very much attention to me during sex, that he didn't check in on me and ask how I was doing. I was the one sharing my man with some girl, in a scene entirely focused on his dick, so he needed to check in. Emotional availability has ever since been at the forefront of my mind when it comes to love and relationships. I may have been an expert of threesomes on film, but I was a novice of threesomes in the bedroom. After that, everything went downhill, including our relationship.

The months of COVID went by painfully slowly. Black Lives Matter happened in the dangerous streets of Los Angeles and across the country, and I lost friendships over the divisive opinions about what was going on in this country. Kelen needed space, and I needed attention. He left on a trip to Palm Springs during the thick of the toilet paper crisis, and I was furious. I took to my Instagram story to vent about being abandoned—that didn't go over well. Kelen wasn't a public person, but I was. COVID did give Kelen and me a wake-up call; we both realized what we wanted out of life, but unfortunately, those things were not the same. As the months of resentment ticked on, I couldn't understand why he was pushing me away, uninterested in rekindling the love we once had. He hadn't been up front with me. He had a plan, and I wasn't in the picture.

Did I manifest this? "You planted seeds of doubt about our relationship, Rachel!" he would often say to me. "I don't know if I ever want to have children!" The fear I had always had sank into my heart. He knew that was all any man would have to say to get me to leave. He begged me to stay at the house when I decided to move out a month before our lease expired. He didn't want to be alone; I declined.

"You can have this place to yourself. The rent is already paid for the month. The one condition is that I can come back and shoot this commercial for my Love Doll," I said as I was leaving this chapter of my life behind.

My Love Doll had recently come out through an online retailer. I was promised that this life-size doll, 3-D scanned from my body and face, would be extremely realistic and incredibly sellable before I signed the contract. I worked for a year on measurements and details with the owner of the company in order to secure a custom doll that looked identical to me for my fans. In theory, fans would buy Tasha 2.0 and hang out with her, play with her, and fuck her. As I departed our cold, austere mansion in the Hollywood Hills, which Kelen thought didn't have a nice enough view, I thought, *How could I have wasted two fucking years of my life?!* That's exactly how I felt—wasteful. I deserved a deep, emotionally available love, a man who wanted a real future with me, not some addict kid from a wealthy family who liked the idea of his girlfriend being a hot porn star. I deserved more.

The day came for me to shoot my commercial. I unboxed the doll and was horrified. The materials that were supposed to be used were nowhere in sight. What I unboxed instead was a botched version of my alter ego, Tasha. She looked very masculine and cheap. I called the manufacturer immediately. "Oh, we stopped using the more realistic materials to create the dolls, but if you want, we can discontinue yours." I had spent thousands of dollars producing the most creative commercial, hiring a videographer, a production assistant, hair and makeup artists, and most importantly, a male talent. I was still going to shoot this commercial. As I got into glam, I had no doubt that the day would go more smoothly, but I was wrong. We shot a cute, scripted video about my clone and me, how to use her, and an introduction to the new doll. Then we got to the back-and-forth dialogue between myself and my coworker, Ramone.

I got a text from Kelen. "Who's that chump?" He had been spying through our front cameras and was not happy. Apparently, I was allowed to use the house I had paid for to shoot a video, but only as long as male talent wasn't there. I had no idea about this rule. He didn't let up. Throughout the day he kept texting me, bugging me, and making my life so stressful that I could barely concentrate. I couldn't believe he had the audacity to live in our house without me, but I couldn't use it to film something PG-rated for Instagram. It felt like an incredibly petty move. I was not surprised. I continued to shoot anyway. For the last scene, we shot Ramone pretending to have sex with my doll. When I heard Kelen's car coming into the driveway, I panicked. "Ramone, quick quick hide in the closet!" as my doll's head bobbed back and forth from the faux intercourse. He did his best. I apologized to Kelen because he seemed so upset and gave him one last hug as his girlfriend. This was not the note I wanted to leave our relationship on. Ultimately the lack of desire to procreate was the real deal breaker for me. I don't think many relationships can progress if one partner doesn't want children and the other does.

I've always loved an intellectual man, someone who can challenge me and keep my interest throughout a conversation. I met Neil Strauss while recording as a guest on his show *Inner Circle*, while he was newly engaged to his fiancée, Ingrid, who sat next to him at the filming of the show. He had gathered an eclectic group of people in a cabin by the beach. There was a gifted saxophonist, a bondage specialist leading a polyamorous life, a few other curious characters, and me. I was attracted to Neil right away; he can really command a room. The interview was odd. He asked me questions about sex work and implied I was escorting in Monaco when that photo of Bill Clinton and me posing at dinner was taken. I most certainly was escorting at the time, although not with Bill Clinton. God forbid I admit that truth. In the porn world, to admit you escort publicly or even privately was still taboo, so I fiercely defended myself. "No, I was there as a guest of *Penthouse*, that's it!" Never in my wildest dreams did I think of saying, *yes, I was there with a client*. I hadn't many complaints about him, and I don't think other women did, either; he was always sweet and really kind to me. I had given little thought at the time to powerful men using their positions to get women to do what they wanted . . . He paid us well; he took us on memorable adventures and always seemed interested in me as a person, but the shame of saying, "Yes, I am paid on occasion to have sex with him or men in general outside of making movies for everyone else to watch," was too much to bear.

I didn't think much of that night in the years to come. I concluded that Neil was off-limits, as he was getting married. Years went by, and I connected with our mutual friend Michael Ellsberg, a writer and interesting man. I told him I was looking for love and to start my family but that I was having a challenge finding the right person to do that with.

"I know just the guy! He wants more children, and he is financially stable," he said. "Neil Strauss!" My heart and mind started to race with excitement as I remembered having a connection the first time we met many years before. Michael put us in a group chat, and Neil asked me to meet him at the Soho House in Malibu, an exclusive members-only club on the ocean. I eagerly said yes and planned my outfit for the night. I thought it was just him and me meeting up, but it was actually a group of what I felt were his fans but maybe his friends as well. He seemed to love to be surrounded by diverse groups of people. We kissed that night across the street at a little Mexican bar. I wasn't necessarily physically attracted to him, but I loved his mind. I have always had a thing for nerds or guys I perceive to be dorky, and Neil was pretty nerdy to me. In his Tesla, he played the intro to a new podcast he was releasing, *To Live and Die in LA*, then dropped me off at my house, about fifteen minutes away in the mountainside. He texted every day and we made plans to hang out pretty frequently, to go to nice dinners and chill at his house.

Dating him was enjoyable, but I was dating multiple men and my heart was leaning toward another, so we went our separate ways for a couple of years.

For some reason, whenever I am single, I think of Neil, of reaching out and connecting with him. He makes me feel safe and secure. I thought he would be the perfect candidate for the father of my children. So I asked Neil to meet me at Mastro's Ocean Club, a restaurant down my street. I told him why I had broken up with Kelen and how badly I wanted children. He empathized with me, and I headed to his house for a little make-out session.

That session led to a deeper conversation about him possibly becoming the sperm donor for my future baby. He already had one child and wanted more. I seriously considered the option, and after getting opinions from family members and friends, I invited him and his son over for dinner. When we spoke about more children, he seemed enthusiastic about the prospect. But when I was clear about my expectation regarding money and possibly an emotional relationship, he was out. He wanted access to this possible child, but what I clearly wanted was a partner. I wanted so much more than a sperm donor out of him.

When I realized Neil was not my best option, I did exactly what my mom did . . . I went to a sperm bank. If I was going to have total control over when and how my baby was going to be conceived, then I was just going to have to do it this way. I didn't feel like I had a second left to spare. I wanted to be a mother, more than anything. I found a sperm bank associated with UCLA and explained to the doctor that I wanted to get pregnant ASAP. She encouraged IVF, which is more costly but more effective. "I'll try intrauterine insemination first," I said. I hoped I could get pregnant that way. It's cheaper and easy on the body, so I all I had to do was take some hormone shots and pick the sperm.

"Is it a difficult choice? How do you do it? Is there a catalog of men, and do you get to choose what they look like?" Everyone kept asking me these questions, probably because they didn't know anyone else who had done this. I mean, the only person I know who has is my mom, and she hid it for seventeen years. There is clearly shame in admitting that you can't find a partner but you feel too old to wait any longer. As I browsed the websites for a sperm donor, I aimed for a tall, handsome man who had many accolades and a positive attitude. You can only tell so much from someone's bio, but I felt good about the sperm I purchased.

I waited until my ovulation cycle, and after many days of getting a shot full of hormones in my belly, I got to be inseminated. "The inseminator," clearly a device some man made up, was administered to me by the doctor. It was painful and stressful. I could barely take the tool being shoved up me, it felt so archaic. "Why does the medical industry not use silicone yet?" I thought as I was being poked and prodded on a table in the middle of the room.

"Now lay there for fifteen minutes," the doctor said as I was left with the sperm in my uterus, hopefully making its way up to create life.

It didn't take.

Round two seemed so far away. *I really have to wait another month?* I thought as I read the pink line on my negative pregnancy test. Bummer city. How come all these teens get pregnant and don't even want kids? But here I was desperately ready and so wanting to become a mom that I was paying for sperm, and it wasn't taking. What a nightmare.

The second round took. I was fucking pregnant! I couldn't believe it. I couldn't believe that I was a pregnant lady, with a baby inside of me, and I was going to be a mom. It was incredible.

Until it wasn't. I was in disbelief. My IUI had worked, and I was actually pregnant. "Rachel, I have some bad news. Your pregnancy is not viable," my doctor told me over the phone. Not viable? How on earth could she know that? "The tests came back, and they show that the HCG [human chorionic gonadotropin, often called the pregnancy hormone] is not growing fast enough for this pregnancy to be viable." My whole world was crumbling down. The worst feeling of my entire life was losing my unborn baby at five weeks old.

"How could it be? I am pregnant . . . so, am I going to miscarry? But when? Will it hurt? Can I get pregnant again?" The questions just kept coming, and my disbelief in the news I was processing would not cease.

In the summer of 2021, I miscarried my first pregnancy. I had no idea I could feel so much pain over the loss of someone I had never met. It felt like I was dying. I would be lying if I told you that my feelings about abortion didn't become messy, because they did. I was a basket case and emotionally drained. When my best friend got pregnant and decided not to keep her baby, I was beside myself. "I'll raise it!" I screamed in agony as she told me she was going to abort it. I convinced myself that I could be its mom. That the baby could be mine. She declined the offer.

My girlfriend and I had started a book club. *Calling in the One* was a how-to book about calling in the love of your life and building the life you want, which my friend Laura had suggested we read together with one other woman. I read most of the book, did most of the worksheets at the end of the chapters, and went about my life. I was still hopeful about finding love. I kept swiping on Hinge, my favorite dating app, as I waited for my next chance to do an IUI. If you've ever tried out the world of dating apps, you'll know that they can be draining and not as romantic as in-person connections. I had enough of the constant right and left, the back-and-forth. Not to mention the constant questioning to myself about whether or not I should be up front about my artificial insemination. I decided one evening that it was time for my typical routine, where I delete the app and then come back again a couple days later. I found one man whom I was very attracted to. At six-five, he was extremely tall and handsome enough to be on the cover of a romance novel. I gave him my number and swiftly deleted the app.

To my surprise, Logan reached out and arranged for a dinner date right away. We were both clearly physically attracted to one another, so we didn't need to talk much for me to realize I wanted to spend time with him. I could use a sexy romp, and he lived nearby. The minute I saw him in person, I felt like I needed to pinch myself, because he was so beautiful that it felt like I was dreaming. He sat across from me at the Draycott in the bougie Palisades Village. I had swiped right on Hinge because of how incredibly handsome he was. Like, drop-dead gorgeous. Logan would make any woman double-take, especially with his beach photos that he had posted in his profile. With long blond locks and baby blue eyes, I was sold the second I saw him. His Texan accent and sweet, disarming demeanor swept me off my feet.

On the third date, I asked him down to Laguna Beach for the Fourth of July weekend with my family. He came with red roses and tons of games for my nephews to play. It was really romantic, because we slept next to a water fountain with the windows open and the breeze blowing in on that warm summer night when we first made love. One night turned into two and then three, and then the entire summer. He was sweet and kind and down-to-earth. He had my heart right away. I wanted so badly to have a baby after my miscarriage, so my emotions were unhinged. Logan wanted to get to know me and take the slower, more traditional route into a family. But how could I go from being shot up with hormones and IUIs for months to just "taking it slow"? I couldn't. I was back to square one.

As the days went by, I told him the details of my fertility

journey. It's not news that most men want to hear when they first start dating: "I have been trying to conceive on my own because I want kids more than I want to wait for love." It's just not an appropriate opener. He seemed perplexed but tried to empathize. As we traveled through Capri and Positano in Italy that summer, I thought I was pregnant. I told Logan that I had missed my period, and to my surprise, he seemed thrilled. Sadly, as he visited the ruins of Pompeii, I was peeing on sticks in the nearby mall bathroom, praying I was pregnant. They don't call it baby fever for nothing! I started my period the next day, and it was there and then we decided to try for a baby.

I was pregnant after our first try, a baby boy! I had life in my womb and hope in my heart. As the hormones began to pump inside of me and my moods became more irritable, I started pushing Logan away. I just couldn't be bothered by anyone, and I wasn't in a good place mentally. I was physically uncomfortable and felt trapped. Going from attempting to conceive on my own to having this man I had to answer to was a change I wasn't prepared for. We barely knew one another, and I was beginning to realize that I might have jumped into things too quickly. I drifted away from Logan, little by little, not reaching out to connect or hang out, and since we didn't live together, that wasn't too difficult to do. I then hired a therapist to help me break it off entirely. I was scared. I felt overwhelmed, and I was very nauseated and hormonal.

But God had a plan. Logan didn't want to break up. He didn't want to repeat the old patterns of our parents, who had had many marriages and divorces and kids from all of them. He asked me out a couple of months later. We went to my favorite old-timey theater in the Pacific Palisades, and we enjoyed each other's company. We slowly began to realize that we should give our love another shot. Not just for us, but for our baby. Logan fought for our family when I was ready to give up. I will never underestimate hormones again. I couldn't have ever imagined that they would impact me the way that they did. The number of things women didn't tell me before I had my son is bewildering. I think it is perhaps one of two things: they forget entirely that any of it happened, or they don't want to scare you away from doing it.

I threw up the entire first trimester of my pregnancy. I broke up with my baby daddy. I thought some unmentionably dark thoughts. I fell into a deep depression, having suicidal ideations, and it was suggested that I get on serious medication, which I declined. It was a roller coaster of emotions.

One morning, a week late for my delivery, I went in for a routine checkup. Upon reading my results, the nurse and doctor informed me that I was going to be induced. My fluid levels were too low to ensure the health of my son, and it was necessary. I ate my last meal, a delicious breakfast sandwich, at Eggslut, my favorite restaurant. I bought a bunch of unnecessary products that I thought I would need at the local drugstore and checked into Cedars-Sinai with a bottle of Veuve Clicquot, genuinely thinking I was going to have a smooth delivery and celebrate at the end.

The next thing I realized was that the Pitocin the nurse had administered was making my baby's heart rate drop, not to mention I had been in labor for thirty-six hours and pushing for six of them. My doula kept track of the time, and my fiancé kept cheering me on. I tried with all my might to push little Luke out vaginally. It turns out when you're short and you have a huge baby, it can be more challenging to have a natural birth. The epidural was a freak show; due to the supply chain and pandemic times, the medication was not on tap but instead administered each time I called the anesthesiologist over into the room. This could take anywhere from twenty minutes to forty-five minutes, depending on the other women who needed it.

"We will need to perform an emergency C-section," my doctor

told us as I wailed in fear of being cut open, wide-awake. I had no idea that this would happen, but I would be lying if I said during that sixth hour of pushing, I wasn't ready for a way out. As I was rolled into the surgery room, I was shaking uncontrollably, another symptom of birth that no one warned me about. "Can you feel this?" the surgeons asked as they used a sharp tool on my belly to test the numbing medicine. "Yes! Yes, I can!" I shouted over the cloth divider. I could feel them, and I didn't want to. "You're not going to be able to remember the birth of your son if we numb you any more . . ." they said as I begged to be sedated.

And just like that, my baby, weighing 8.5 pounds and looking like a real-life cherub, was born. I was hemorrhaging. Severely dehydrated and out of it, I stayed extra nights recovering in the ICU. My son was perfectly healthy, and I was grateful to be alive.

As I write, Luke, my son, is kicking in his bassinet next to me, and he is the best decision I have ever made. Motherhood is my calling. I feel like my life is finally about to start, like my fate, dreams, and desires are all in alignment and everything's right in my world. I have never felt the joy that I feel right now, knowing he is my healthy son. How did we get this lucky?

One day I will have to have difficult conversations with Luke about sex work, about porn, about my past. I will do my absolute best to be his teacher and guide. I will make him a media-literate person. I will raise him to be a man who respects women, specifically sex workers. But for now, I am simply a new mom. This journey has been trying. I am grateful for every single experience and person who has helped me along this tumultuous road to motherhood.

Enthusiastic Consent

Growing up between Laguna and Newport Beach, the University of Southern California meant status. It symbolized importance, a true way to belong in a world that often felt lonely. It felt like it was my destiny. And then my bubble burst when I applied and got denied my senior year of high school, and then again in college after my sophomore year associate of arts degree was completed, and I hoped to transfer to my dream school. Denied. Denied. Denied. My family and ex-boyfriend had rejected me, and now USC. My early twenties felt like a tidal wave that kept crashing down on me.

But then, about a decade later, I had another shot at stepping into my fantasy and saying to the world, "I go to USC!" My aunt Annie, although she didn't say it in so many words, didn't love my career choice. Whether she didn't think it was very safe or had much longevity, she noticed my writing ability and pushed me in the direction of graduate school. Graduate school was something I had thought about but didn't really feel the need to attend. I love being a student, but I was so busy hustling that I hadn't caught my breath to consider the expensive educational investment and time commitment of another degree. Now, with my trust fund available to me, I could afford to stop shooting as much and study writing.

When I applied for the master's program in specialized journalism at USC's Annenberg School for Communication and Journalism, I needed to write a powerful essay that spoke to something I was passionate about: consent. I had been using a lot of my time to speak to fraternity brothers on campuses around California about the importance of consent before sexual activity, so I had really made my brand about how important consent was, and I found that coming from me, a porn star, it had tremendous impact on the students I interacted with. *Would a topic like this be good enough to get me into my dream school?* I thought. Sure, I had written articles for magazines and newspapers with the help of great editors, but would USC validate this topic I was so passionate about? I wrote the essay from Japan. I always do my best writing when I'm not home.

I had invited myself on my girlfriend/coworker's vacation to Japan. I had never been, and it sounded like so much fun. However, from the moment our flight took off, we butted heads. I can't honestly say if I started the bickering or if it was the red wine they were pouring on this flight, but the next thing I knew, my friend and I were screaming and fighting in the parking lot of the pink blossom tree forest, and she walked away. She left me, and she was the only one with reservations at the hotel. She probably figured I was independent enough to book a new hotel, but what in the actual fuckery was this? Were we in middle school? I returned solemnly back to my bed-and-book hostel. I promptly extended my stay and decided this was where I would apply to grad school, in a bunk bed in a room with a bunch of other random strangers in their bunk beds. The place was a book lover's fantasy come to life, with books decorating every inch of the hostel and bookshelves that slid open to reveal bunk beds. For less than one hundred dollars a night, you can feel like you're in another world. I visited lots of recommended spots, and explored owl cafés, the Harajuku fashion district, Japanese nail art, the Piss Alley, and so much more. Between my travels, I wrote. I explained to the acceptance board how my career led me to view consent differently than the average sexually active twentysomething, and how their school had been my favorite institution for as long as I could remember.

To graduate from Annenberg in specialized journalism, every student must submit a thesis, which is available for everyone (outsiders included) to read in their online database. This thesis must be looked over, analyzed, edited, and then eventually approved by a team of three professors. They can be your own, but probably won't be, because they need to correlate with the topic you're doing your thesis on. Students need to research, through asking around and online sources, whom those professors might be. Then you need to ask them if they would be willing to serve as your chairperson or committee member for your entire program over the next two years.

One afternoon in my Sandy Cohens journalism class, my professor suggested I meet with a female professor at USC, because she would be a great addition to my then all-male thesis committee. He had implied he didn't want it to look misogynistic. I agreed, and I reached out to her to set up a meeting. She seemed short via email, which was unsettling, but I figured it was all just par for the course. I met her at a cozy café in Santa Monica. She was shaking and looked extremely anxious. She must have been going through a lot that week. I hadn't really seen a teacher act like this before. She was unfriendly and rude; it was as if she had turned me down without even hearing what I had to say beforehand.

She started our conversation saying that the work I was doing with fraternity brothers, the work I was so proud of, was really just a Band-Aid, something that worked in the short term but wasn't really addressing the root of the issue. I couldn't disagree entirely, as I didn't think my advocacy work alone was the solution to sexual assault, but I felt like it was a step in the right direction. I felt shut down. Then she asked me a question that has haunted me since. "Rachel," she said, "have you ever seen *The Handmaid's Tale*?" I sure had! It was only my favorite feminist show that I quoted regularly and obsessed over with all my friends. "Well, you are like Mrs. Waterford—you are part of the system. Remember when Mrs. Waterford gave Offred the little jewelry box with the dancing ballerina in it? That is basically what you are doing as a privileged woman."

If you haven't seen this show, it takes place in Gilead, a futuristic dystopia where women have limited rights and are there only to create children as handmaids or to serve their husbands, like Mrs. Waterford. She said that I was like Mrs. Waterford, the wife of the home, who also was limited, but had more freedom than the handmaids, who were raped every month. She thought I was a ballerina trapped in a little music box, and that even though my intention was good—to help fraternity brothers become more enlightened about consent—my actual role within the system was still oppressive. That I was simply part of the problem, that ultimately pornography was the trouble and I could never be feminist in my attempt to promote safe and consensual sex.

Was she right? I thought after she declined to be one of my thesis committee members. She might be; I still ponder that thought today. As Audre Lorde once famously said, "For the master's tools will never dismantle the master's house. They may allow us to temporarily beat him at his own game, but they will never enable us to bring about genuine change. Racism and homophobia are real conditions of all our lives in this place and time." I think of this quote often, as it is relevant in our misogynistic, racist, homophobic, whorephobic society today. Although Lorde does not specify women, the quote is very much applicable to the intersectionality of women's roles in today's culture.

Leading up to this meeting, I had been working hard, doing outreach at fraternity houses. Like many young women who walk into frat houses, I had texted several of my girlfriends beforehand to let them know where I would be, so if something happened to me, they would know. I felt nervous that I was about to be surrounded, in an enclosed space, with a bunch of guys from fraternities, often known as bastions of assault and rape.

There was another layer to this situation: In all likelihood, many of these young men had masturbated to images of my nude body. I wasn't there to party with them, though I'd been to plenty of frat parties when I was an undergraduate at UCLA.

I was there to talk to them about consent.

I'm a porn star. By many accounts, I'm one of the biggest names in the industry. You might not think a porn star would care about consent. After all, the stereotype (and video persona) of us is that we're the kind of woman who is always saying yes to everything. So where would the word *no* even come into play?

And you've probably heard stories about how porn is a cause—many people in media even say a major cause—of the crisis of rape and sexual assault on our campuses and beyond.

So what on Earth does a porn star have to say about sexual consent?

It turns out, I had a whole lot to say.

I was standing at a booth signing autographs at the AdultCon porn convention in LA. (For those of you who don't know about porn conventions, think comic or video game conventions, with the same number of young men walking around, except there are no comics or video games, and the "booth babes" are actual porn stars!)

This was my third convention—I'd been in the industry for two years now and was already a huge name—and before this day, nothing bad had ever happened to me at work that I was consciously aware of. For most of these men who come up to get my autograph, meeting the real-life version of the woman whose image has launched a thousand of their orgasms is one of the high points in their life to date. Rather than being aggressive or disrespectful, most of these men seem like giddy kids meeting their favorite sports star or pop star.

But not this man.

As I handed him the poster I had just signed for him, he literally grabbed me by the pussy—he scooped his hand up my stretchy dress and took a hard squeeze.

I still have a somatic memory of the shock that overtook my whole body. "What the FUCK are you doing?" I yelled at him.

"What are you going to do about it?" he taunted, then sauntered off.

I wish I could say I went to get a security guard, so that he wouldn't assault any other women at the convention (which he may very well have done). But, as is common for victims of sexual assault, especially when it's the first time, I froze. I went numb. I didn't know what to feel or think. I think I must have signed a few more autographs after that, but honestly, I have no recollection, I was so in my head.

And then, five minutes later, my assailant was in front of my face again.

"Tasha, do you remember what I did to you?" He stood there, taunting me. "You know you wanted it. You loved it, didn't you?"

Now I was in double shock that, after such a brazen attack, he would come right back and shove it in my face.

I turned to the "bodyguard" at the booth, and asked him, "Aren't you going to do anything?" (I put "bodyguard" in quotes because, while there should have been a real bodyguard at the booth—just like legions of celebrities have around them while amid throngs of fans—this guy wasn't a legit bodyguard. He was just some sketchy dude Devon sent to "look after" us girls at the booth.)

The "bodyguard" looked at me, with my assailant standing only a few feet away from me making nasty faces, and said, "All the other girls at the convention are letting guys do that to them."

Then my attacker looked me right in the eyes and repeated in the most demeaning tone he possibly could, "What are you going to do about it?"

A switch flipped inside of me, and with a louder voice I finally threatened, "I am going to get security!"

He bolted away as quickly as he had appeared. I froze in my booth. Like so many sexual assault survivors, I couldn't speak, I couldn't move. I just kept replaying that horrible event in my head and—as is common among survivors—trying to figure out if I had somehow "caused" it. Had I asked for it? Had I lost my right to speak up about sexual assault because I was a "whore"? This was not how I was raised.

I was raised to speak out about any kind of sexual harassment. I felt I had let that upbringing down; I hadn't lived up to what I was supposed to do. There's a burden on women to say something when something bad happens. But in the moment, it was different. I simply froze.

I didn't know what to do, because nothing quite like this had ever happened to me. Not a day goes by that I don't think of this trauma and wish I had reacted more quickly and assertively. Even though it was almost a decade ago, and I know that my participation in the adult industry doesn't mean I deserve to be assaulted, the guilt and self-slut-shaming refuses to quit haunting me.

I consider myself to be a solution-oriented person. If there is an issue worth fighting for, I will fight. If there is a problem, I will try to solve it.

I realized the concept of consent is unclear to many American men. I decided it was time for me to help fix that.

I was a junior at UCLA when the assault happened. I was majoring in women's studies—inspired by the feminism of sex-positive pioneers in the adult industry such as Nina Hartley and jessica drake.

Around this time, a professor of psychology there reached out to my publicist and asked if I could give a guest lecture in one of his classes. I decided that I wanted to educate these students about the relationship between consent and the porn they were (likely) viewing.

I started by talking about how porn viewers often think of a porn set as if it's some kind of wild Roman orgy where everyone is drunk and anything goes, where porn stars are deemed unrapeable. What they don't realize is that—on a professional porn set at least, the kind I advocate to work on or produce—it's the opposite. There is vastly more prenegotiation of boundaries and consent than occurs in the typical college party hookup. That doesn't mean there's not massive room for improvement in the prenegotiation on porn sets and in the porn culture in general. On the contrary, porn is finally having a major #MeToo reckoning, years after the reckoning started with #MeToo in Hollywood. Artists like Stoya spoke out even before the #MeToo in Hollywood movement had taken off.

But compared to the abysmal amount of presex consent conversation that occurs during the typical alcohol-fueled party hookup, any prenegotiation before sex is miles ahead.

On a professional porn shoot, there's an (increasingly detailed) discussion of what will and won't happen on the scene. For example, shoots that feature anal sex usually pay 50 to 100 percent more than just vaginal sex, so that part has already been negotiated in the contract. (This is so different than off-screen sex, in which it's not uncommon for some guys to just try to "slip it in" the butt, with no discussion.)

And if it's a fetish/kink/BDSM shoot, on any reputable set, the parameters of that have already been negotiated: safe words, which performers can use to immediately stop the action, plus what type of activity will take place and implements will be used (rope, chains, floggers, ball gags, etc.)

But even in a vanilla (nonkink) shoot, there are more subtle boundaries that are increasingly discussed beforehand, particularly around sex that isn't BDSM-style, but that could be described as rough sex: Choking? Slapping? Spanking? Hair pulling?

Trade groups for the industry, such as the APAC, are disseminating, normalizing, and encouraging the use of consent checklists and a "Performer Bill of Rights" ahead of time to make sure everyone is on the same page about what is and is not going to happen. While I don't necessarily think consent forms are a good idea for off-set, civilian (nonprofessional) hookups, I do think that the civilian world would do well to learn from the degree of detail that goes into prenegotiating sexual scenes.

People in the civilian world are often worried that prenegotiating boundaries will "kill the mood" or lessen the hotness. The irony is, the very porn they consume has been preceded by prenegotiation—and it certainly doesn't reduce the hotness once the action starts! My discussion of these topics in the UCLA psychology class segued into a theme that has been the center of my consent education and activism since—people see crazy, rough, wild, aggressive sex scenes in porn and don't see all the communication that—hopefully—went on behind the scenes to make that safe and consensual. Then some people, especially guys, start thinking it's normal to just slap or choke their partner out of nowhere in the middle of sex. When they do that, their partner feels violated or assaulted. And then people see porn as the culprit. The real culprit is that our nation has effectively zero education for young people about how to properly establish consent before sex.

While many people blame porn performers, I actually believe that porn performers can and should be a source of the solution— by educating the public about just how much consent should go on behind the scenes, and how it should be established. We should lift the curtain behind the scenes—because what we do behind the curtain is exactly what most people should be doing before engaging in sex. It is our expertise, so who better to ask?

My lecture at UCLA was wildly popular with the students. Most of them (particularly the men) look at porn, and they were insatiably curious about what goes on behind the scenes.

When they learned that what goes on behind the scenes is not—as they had imagined—a wild bacchanal, but rather, a much more detailed discussion about consent than they likely ever had during their drunken Saturday-night hookups, they wanted to know more.

They were much more interested in learning about consent from a porn star than from some boring bureaucratic educator their college administration had sent their way. Invitations for lectures came in from UC San Diego and Chapman University in Orange County, all of which I obliged. I was even invited to speak as a keynote speaker at the University of Oregon.

Then I received an invitation that I never would have imagined— but that made perfect sense. A fraternity brother at AEPi, the Jewish fraternity at UCLA, attended one of my class lectures and asked me if I could talk to the new brothers at his frat about consent.

Now, talking to a frat about consent might seem like talking to bar patrons about the need for alcohol moderation, or a BBQ party about the need for eating vegetables. But it's also exactly the audience that needs to hear it—and that's why I said yes.

Like many women who are sexual assault survivors, I felt nervous walking into a frat. Not that I had any specific reason to believe that the AEPi brothers were themselves dangerous. But the overall concept of a frat does not have a good ring to a woman concerned about sexual assault.

Which is precisely why it was necessary for me to talk there. It was also why these forward-looking brothers—looking to improve their culture, and the reputation of frats in general—invited me.

I dressed in a lacy green romper. It was not overly sexualized, which I don't think would have been the right tone. But wasn't frumpy, either—it hugged my curves. I knew that a lot of the reason these men were going to pay attention was because they were attracted to me. I had no problem using that edge if it was going to get them to listen and learn. (I'd been using that edge for more frivolous ends my whole life!)

Upon arrival at AEPi, I was greeted with big smiles, a bouquet of flowers, and a group of respectful young adults. What a relief! There was even a woman or two (house moms?) walking around the halls of the big house. My fears melted away, and I became enthusiastic to talk to these men. The brothers were dressed in white attire, and there was a candle lit as I entered a special room at the top floor. People not familiar with fraternities or sororities on campus may not know just how integral ceremony and ritual are to Greek life. I was impressed that these brothers had pulled out all the stops for me.

As I looked around the room and stared at the freshman fraternity brothers, I said, "My name is Tasha Reign, and I want to talk about sex and consent today with you. I know most of you watch adult films, and I am afraid your parents and education haven't sufficiently prepared you for having real conversations with your partners about consent. Let me clear some things up."

I passed around pens and paper for them to write down their questions about sex and asking permission, anonymously. I felt this was important, because I imagined they might not feel comfortable admitting lack of knowledge around sexual affairs, or showing sexual vulnerability, in front of their brothers.

The three most common questions I received from them—not only at this first event but at the many similar talks I subsequently gave at fraternities across California—were some versions of the following:

1. "How do I ask for consent in a sexy way, without ruining the moment?"

2. "How can I get consent if I'm drunk, or the girl is drunk?"

3. "What if a girl makes up that I sexually assaulted or raped her?"

Here's how I answered these questions:

1. I find it sexy when a man asks me for permission. Of course, asking, "Can I put my hand here?" can be done in a way that feels unconfident (which is a turn-off) or confident (which is a turn-on). But there, the issue is confidence, not the act of asking.

A man who is confident is likely going to be attractive to a lot of women no matter what, and asking for permission only makes him more attractive. (Because it shows that he has the confidence to risk rejection.) A man who is not confident is likely not going to be attractive to many women—so it's really not the asking that's the issue.

You can practice asking for a woman's permission to touch her (use a mirror!) just like you might practice asking a woman out on a date. In fact, they're pretty much the same thing. You don't just corral a woman and force her to go to dinner and a movie with you—you ask her first!

But either way, whether you're confident or not, you have to make sure that she actually wants to be doing what you're doing. And you're by far most likely to know that by asking; relying on what you hope she wants, or what you think she wants, can go wrong in too many ways.

When a guy checks in with me during intercourse—"Can I touch here?" "How does that feel?" "Is this good for you?"—that shows me he cares about my pleasure and well-being, and that's a huge turn-on. You can potentially do the acts with your partner that you have always dreamed of if you vocalize the desire to do so. The power of the voice is so important, and oftentimes men are not socialized to use it.

Most guys aren't used to hearing a woman whom they lust after tell them they prefer when guys ask first. I hope that my example sways their mind on this and gets them to think about it in a new way.

2. When thinking about alcohol and consent, a good analogy is alcohol and driving. A few drinks spaced out over an evening, and you're likely to be below the blood alcohol content for safe driving. But if you get over the BAC—which usually happens pretty fast in a night of partying—not only are you breaking the law if you drive, but worse, you could injure or kill yourself or others. Is that really worth it?

It's possible that when you meet and hook up with a woman, when one or both of you is drunk, you're both going to be enthusiastic about it and feel great about it the next day when you're sober. But it's also possible you're going to get into a consent car wreck.

Why risk it, for her, or for you? Is hooking up with a stranger so important that it must be done that very night, when you're both wasted? If you like her enough to want to hook up with her, why not get her number and see her the next day, when you're both sober?

All of this becomes even more relevant when you're drinking underage, just as it is for driving. Not only is the behavior riskier when you have less life experience, but the law looks at it as much more serious if you're below twenty-one and have a car wreck, or a consent wreck, when you've been drinking against the law.

Also, I tell men—as someone who has certainly had far more sex than they have: sex is better when you're both coherent and can trust your partner. All you need to do is wait one day until you're both sober, to make it much safer for you and your partner. Are you so desperate for an immediate hookup that you need to take these risks?

3. More and more colleges are adopting affirmative consent (asking for permission) as the standard by which to judge if sexual activity was consensual. Whether you agree with that standard or not, it's likely the rule in your very school. And either way, it's become the rule culturally now. Why not just follow the rule?

It's extremely unlikely that someone is going to lie and say you didn't ask when in fact you did ask. Your risk of false accusations—which statistics show is already extremely low even without affirmative consent rules in place—drops to near zero. The rules protect you as well as her. Everyone wins.

Overall, I found the young men in these fraternity education sessions to be open-minded and receptive about what I was sharing with them. They were curious and excited about pleasing women. Only a few times would a man make it known that he was not interested or thought that what I was talking about wasn't important to him.

For the first time, they experienced an in-the-flesh woman, whom most of them likely viewed as extremely sexually attractive (and had possibly even masturbated to), telling them that the things she wanted from a man were actually aligned with the things that would keep both them and other women safe.

The men were effusive in their thanks. They'd never been given this information before, at least not from a person that was likely to grab their attention and make them listen. They'd never had a space to talk honestly about their concerns and ask their questions with a person whose experience on these matters they trusted.

The fraternity heads called up multiple other fraternities and told them they needed to get me in there ASAP to share this information with them. Soon, I had been invited to speak at other schools, including AEPi at UC Santa Barbara, UC San Diego, and Cal State Fullerton. My inbox was now full of invitations from frats across the country, and I was expanding my outreach to young men, eager to learn about consent, as fast as I could.

My dear friend the writer Michael Ellsberg had wanted to team up together and go on a tour, spreading our message on a larger scale. The interfraternity council accepted his proposed fee for his services. However, when I asked to be paid for the work I was going to continue to do, they quickly shut me down. Claiming that because I hadn't charged them before, they weren't going to pay me for something I was originally doing for free. The patriarchy, go figure.

At the same time, I launched my career as one of the leading voices trying to make porn, and porn stars, a force for educating young men about consent.

My efforts were featured on Lisa Ling's CNN *This Is Life* series (season six, episode one, "Porn Ed"), on *The Daily Beast*, and on CNN's *Across America With Carol Costello*. Almost immediately I got messages from the presidents of each fraternity stating that I was no longer welcome at their houses because the interfraternity council did not approve of the way it made them "look." The irony here was not lost on me.

I don't believe it's the porn industry's job to provide adequate sex education (any more than it's Hollywood's job to provide adequate education about proper gun use, responsible driving, moderation of drugs and alcohol, or how to have emotionally healthy relationships). Porn and Hollywood are entertainment industries, not education industries, and in entertainment, that which is out of the ordinary (i.e., fantasy) sells. Fantasy is not reality.

However, the total abdication by parents and schools of even a pretense of trying to educate young people about sex, and their proactive hiding of information about sex from kids (whether out of morality or just plain old embarrassment) has meant that young people seek out information about sex wherever they can get it. And that wherever tends to be internet porn.

While I don't believe it's our duty to take on the sex education function that parents and schools have unconscionably abandoned, I do believe we have an opportunity to play that role, and it's an opportunity we should relish. After all, who are college kids more likely to listen to—their parents, or some consent consultant brought in by administrators . . . or a porn star?

Furthermore, one duty the media, parents and the education system have is to educate the public about the difference between their misconceptions of how porn itself is made versus the realities behind the scenes. If schools could implement this by hiring sex educators to speak on pornography, it would allow for students to become educated, informed, critical consumers as adults. Or more importantly for the conversation about sex to happen way before these adolescents discover internet porn. When asked by friends of mine who have children how to keep their kids safe from internet porn, I always say 1. Install porn blocking software on any device you have control of. 2. Have the sex conversations well before there is a chance that your child will try to learn about sex through adult material intended for adults, like internet porn. If we, as a society, could normalize the relationship we have with the adult business, it would also allow there to be a partnership between producers, performers, and consumers, in making the industry whose products we consume ethical and safe for all involved.

As part of this wider education, I believe it's necessary for us in the porn industry to be honest with the public about the ugly side of porn production as it currently stands. We are loath to do that, because the industry is already under so much legal and cultural attack from fundamentalists and the antiporn wing of the feminist movement. We do not wish to give our adversaries additional ammo for their attacks on our very livelihood and expression.

While that's an understandable impulse, it's no longer viable. As of 2020, porn is finally undergoing a long-overdue reckoning. (In the wake of the George Floyd murder, the industry—like most industries—is also starting a long-overdue effort to root out entrenched racism within the industry. As a white woman, I am not a leader on these efforts but a student and a follower, and I gratefully acknowledge and support the courageous leadership of Black people in the industry.)

The porn industry is famous for being an early adopter of new technology, from photography to film to home video to Internet video to VR. Unfortunately, in moral terms, the industry has been a late adopter to the kinds of worker protections, #MeToo changes, and racial reckonings that we are seeing now in most other industries.

In the realm of worker protections and #MeToo, my life's work has transitioned into helping change that. To normalize the adult business and the incredibly talented artists who are at the core of it. And I'm thrilled to report that it's finally happening on a wider scale in the industry, with lots of room to grow. I hope the next generation of adult performers continues to chip away at the oppression within the business, instead experiencing ultimate freedom by means of independent content creation and better working conditions. Additionally, I hope that women in this business are believed when they speak out against predators. Tired of hearing what other people think of porn and porn stars, I wanted to tell you my own story . . . the good, the bad, and the ugly!

Epilogue

I hope you enjoyed my most intimate tales and that you are encouraged to do something daring. Something bold. Something heretical. I also want to confide something in you . . . I wrote this book with the intention of telling you my unique story, through my lens. But what happened instead was a very therapeutic experience. I was able to drop the weight that I have been carrying around with me. Confronting some of these truths has given me peace, so I thank you for listening. I also want to affirm that I do LOVE the adult business with a big part of my heart, even if it's broken my heart once or twice. I hope that shines through in my writing.

While I was writing this book, my mother died from a drug overdose.

Musings

If being an adult film actress teaches you anything, it teaches you about empathy. As soon as you obtain your scarlet letter after you make your first adult film, you are automatically judged in a way that you never were before. You may have been a wild teen in high school or in college. You may have taken nude photos or discreetly dabbled in sex work. But there is something transformative about being seen in this particular light, where people feel like they know you. People feel like they have seen everything and therefore they are entitled to this very narrow, very specific opinion of who you are, what you are, and why you do what you do.

It sounds dramatic, right? But it's true. There is a certain patriarchal gaze that people see through when they view me through a "porn star lens," and, shocker . . . it isn't flattering. Most people automatically assume you have daddy issues and that you are looking for validation through sex. But I would say many women have emotional baggage around their relationship with their parents and look for validation through work, or social media, or other avenues, but they are not pigeonholed and shamed about it the way we are.

When my little sister discovered online that I was making movies, she was horrified. What she was most flabbergasted by was that they were with other women. "Rachel is making lesbian porn!" she told my mom. I was not thrilled for my mom to find out about this sensitive topic through other people. I wanted to tell her myself, in a way that was more thoughtful. My mom was getting creepy emails from my stepmother with links to my sex videos; Darcy was making cruel statements about me and my newfound reputation. My own mother was writing messages to me about how disgusting it was that "now your uncles and cousins can see your vagina." No one wants to hear that kind of commentary from their mom. My stepbrother shamed me. "Guys at school are making fun of me now, because of you!!" All my twenty-one-year-old self heard was "You're a fucking whore!"

My own girlfriends slowly started to distance themselves from me, and I felt more and more isolated. Friends said, "What are you going to do after this?" They implied no one would want me after I have been used up in the porn world. Friends said, "Rachel seems like she's on something, doesn't she? Her voice doesn't seem like her, in her videos." They told me I was deeply confused and lying to myself about my own career. "That's a farce that you feel empowered. You're going down a horrible path." Friends didn't invite me to their birthdays anymore. I received text messages like, "My family feels so badly for you." I felt ostracized. I had guys texting me about sex, things like, "I didn't know that you liked getting fucked!" or even making fun of me at hometown parties, moaning sex sounds at me as I walked past. It was one of the loneliest times in my life.

The thing about shame is that once you internalize it, it's difficult to shake off. For instance, if you're told over and over again that you're beautiful, then you may start to think that is true. If you're told over and over again that you're worthless and should be ashamed, then you may start to believe that, too. It is nearly impossible to ignore what people are saying about you, especially when it is backed up on television, in movies, through social media, and even the news. The most challenging part about doing porn is what other people think about you. Once I became a sex worker, it was impossible not to notice the extreme ways in which women are slut-shamed in our culture. It was impossible not see the way mainstream movies have been portraying women all this time, right in front of our faces. Being a bisexual woman myself, I see a parallel to the way that society sometimes speaks about gay or sexually fluid people—as a threat to be avoided.

Media literacy is another factor in thinking about content in a healthy way. America notoriously has poor sex education. Even worse is our education surrounding pornography. It would only make sense if we learned in high school about porn in a similar manner that we learn about sex, drugs, and alcohol. So why don't we? Porn is a unique niche of entertainment that is difficult to define as a performer. Society won't let you say you're a model, although you're most certainly modeling, and Hollywood won't let you say you're an actress, although you're definitely acting. And *porn star* sounds degrading due to decades of discrimination and false narratives being perpetuated. *Performer*, to me, is the most appropriate word to use while defining my craft.

Things I would tell new talent:

Your story is important and unique.

What other people say might not matter, but there are lifelong consequences that will unfortunately linger and may prevent you from doing other things you want to do, like teaching elementary school children.

Sex work is valid and important. Try to control your work situation. If that means working for yourself, then work for yourself. If it means spending money up front, spend it. Keeping yourself safe will be your secret to a long-lasting career.

Own everything associated with your name, your website, your brand, your image.

Don't ever feel like you're asking for too much. If you want the set to be cleaner, ask for it to be cleaned. If you don't want a creepy location owner to spy on you while you shoot, throw a fucking fit—you're worth it. Whatever you think your rate should be, voice that, and don't let anyone lower your standards. Be on time. I have had plenty of shoots where I showed up late. It's not a good look. Hydrate. Speak up if you're uncomfortable or abused. Call the police, file a report, get a lawyer, don't let anyone tell you that it's just part of the job. It is not. Be hygienic; this is the key to attraction for many people. Just make sure that you're showered and smelling good.

Be healthy in mind, body, and spirit. This will be important for you to maintain your peace.

Never be ashamed of self-promotion. It's vital. There is no guarantee that the money will come, so make sure you're not just doing it for the money.

MILFs

In porn, you are either a teen or you're a MILF (mom I'd like to fuck). The in-between is really nonexistent. You can try your hardest to grasp roles as a glam girl, which is a short-lived period of time in porn where you're not quite a girl but not yet a woman—but honestly, you have to hold onto that for dear life, and the control you have over what the director titles the movie is limited. The chances of them naming you a MILF in a movie if you're over twenty-five are very high. Does art reflect life, or does life reflect art? In real life, how much time are women given between being a teen and being pressured to become a mom? Not very much time at all. You have a quick life of being a glam girl, and then boom, it's time to grow up.

If you're like me and your dream is to become a mom, but you're constantly being called a MILF without having children yet, it's utterly painful. The age in California for becoming a mom is not usually twenty-five; on average, it's thirty-two, so I really feel like this rule of thumb should be adjusted. Why is it that teens and MILFs are the most popular and largest genres in the adult industry? Is it the Freudian theory that we are all attracted to our opposite-sex parent, or is it that underneath the polished images we have fantasies of young girls? Or maybe it's the nostalgia for teenage years, which are many people's highlight reel. Whatever it is, I have always wished that porn would let us just be women.

I've always wanted to be perfect. I'm not going to blame that on my mom, the media, or Laguna Beach, but maybe a combination of them all created a clinically diagnosed perfectionist. The adult industry exacerbated that mental health issue for me, because of the millions of people watching me. The pressure to be sexually attractive and compete with other women was heightened to an extreme no twentysomething should have to deal with. I like to compare the adult business to a beauty pageant, and I have participated in a couple of pageants, so I can say that with accuracy. There is a desire to compete with other women in our society at large, and then in pornography, there is an even smaller group of women competing for the attention, the work, the recognition, and the awards.

Imagine that the younger and stereotypically prettier you are, the more your literal financial worth is. This attribute gets you booked for jobs. And it's not just beauty, but like in a pageant, there are skill sets you need to master. Are you easy to work with? Are you in shape? Can you do scenes with many people involved? Are you a good actor with dialogue? Can you perform? In the adult industry, "perform" means just how entertaining it is to watch you fuck on film. You might think you're good in bed, but that is entirely different from how well you perform on screen and with strangers. There is just so much pressure, especially for performers who may be as young as eighteen. Then you are put up against other women who look similar to you to fight for the limited roles on set. It was all very overwhelming for me, and I was used to competition. To make matters worse, I still feel that same heavy weight on my shoulders even though my life has changed so drastically. I find myself scrolling Instagram, feeling the fear of missing out, and comparing, comparing, comparing.

Sexual harassment and unsafe work conditions make the pressure to be perfect even worse in the adult business. If you're not perfect, you're not a pleasure to work with on set. And you're not a pleasure to work with on set if you're not compliant. If you're not comfortable with the director sexually abusing you, the creepy homeowner watching your production, or your agent taking advantage of you, are you a perfect performer?

It was only recently that I realized that what makes me unique, what makes me authentically special, is that I am imperfect. I have my own story, and while it might not be exactly how I would have wanted it to be, my experience is messy, and it's mine. That knowledge has sparked within me the desire to be deeply authentic, true, genuine, and someone who doesn't hide the truth. That is why I wrote this book—to speak my truth and encourage others to speak theirs.

At home in Laguna Beach, I wanted to be perfect. At the *Playboy* Mansion, I needed to be perfect. In porn, perfectionism was also necessary in order for me to maintain my career. Now, at thirty-two, I am finally willing to give up the perfect act. This book is dedicated to anyone who feels society's immense pressure to seem perfect to everyone else.

Henry David Thoreau said, "All good things are wild and free." This quote speaks to my inner soul. I first heard of the founding father of libertarian thought, Thoreau, in a philosophy class at Santa Monica Community College, and thought, *Wow, that's a unique way to view the world.* I didn't necessarily identify with being a libertarian, but I felt strongly about living life on my own terms and in my own way. I had always hated rules, social standards, having to behave a certain way just because I was a woman. I felt like people's view of sexualized women was all wrong—I really wanted to be free. There was a part of me that liked the rebellious feeling I got when I engaged in behavior that was socially unacceptable. The attention I got from men and women made me feel special and important. I was attracted to being in *Playboy* because I identified as a rebel, a thought I never had until I watched A&E's recent documentary series *Secrets of the Playboy Mansion*.

Hugh M. Hefner appealed to the side of me that thought freedom was more important than all else. He attracted educated, polished, refined women who wanted a place and a community to call home. All of us had a mutual understanding of doing what we wanted, when we wanted, and how we wanted to do it.

Hef's philosophy about freedom and sexuality had me hooked. It was the reason I gave in interviews for wanting to be a part of *Playboy*. I identified and still identify as a feminist. I'm not a radical feminist, an antisex feminist, and maybe not even a traditional feminist, but I thought that working for Hef and being a part of his world made me a more serious feminist. Aside from the judgment I constantly got from outside forces, I was doing something that brought me happiness and, although I constantly had to defend my career choice, I felt empowered.

The word *empowerment* was used a lot throughout the *Playboy* docuseries and throughout my young adult life. It is a word that can easily lead someone to think they are doing something of their own free will, when in fact they may be just carrying out the views of a cultlike group. More and more, it has been clear to me that my two-year or so involvement at the *Playboy* Mansion was not as freeing as I once thought. Even if my own personal experience there was mostly benevolent, the masses of women who have been courageous enough to speak up about their trauma and negative experiences at the *Playboy* Mansion have led me to seriously reconsider the moments I cherished at Hef's house.

The documentary made me reconsider that idea of freedom, feminism, and Hugh Hefner as a person—specifically, what he stood for and how he manipulated women for his own personal gain. Was my identity as a sex-positive feminist all a farce? Was I perpetuating a false narrative? No. But it's safe to say that it was wrapped up in a misogynist idea of what feminism and empowerment was. I can say that now, but at the time, I was vehemently defensive of the accusation coming from anyone else. Looking back at when I was kicked out of the Mansion for my "hard-core" movies, that should have been an indicator my image was being controlled. But instead, I was just really sad that Hef had personally banished me. *Why me?* I thought as I read Hef's letters over and over again. I was working hard, making money, being sexually independent and liberated from society's standards of what was acceptable. He should have been proud of me if he was truly about libertarianism.

Just because my personal experience of being indoctrinated into *Playboy* culture involved being hand-painted for parties, modeling for spreads, eating dinner with Hef and the girls, movie nights, pool days, and everything in between, and was mostly fun and innocent in nature, doesn't take away from the fact that tons of women are finally coming forth and speaking their truth with harrowing stories of Hef back in the day. One of the reasons my overall recollection of this time in my life was so pleasant is because he was dating, and eventually married, Crystal, his widow, who kept the social chaos and partying to a minimum. He was starting to get ill or fade away due to age and health, and that also dictated the energy and the mood of the house. He was less able to abuse, control, and stir up drama at that time in his life.

* * *

The pressure to be formally educated was always on my mind. When so many people called me names online and the media encouraged people to believe that adult stars were stupid, my desire to be able to say, "I have my master's degree from Annenberg," grew. I have always battled with the inner dichotomy of caring what people think of me versus not caring about what people think of me. Attending fancy schools was my way of proving everyone wrong.

"Is the money really good?" must be the one of the main questions civilians ask me. That and "How does your job affect your sex life?" The answer is that income varies drastically for each performer during different stages in their career. I can say that if you're eighteen years old and a woman, the money will probably be better than most jobs. But to maintain your star power and relevancy is not only a full-time job, but a risky one.

The second question is even more nuanced. People ask whether I am actively performing or haven't in many years. It is as if because I made adult films in my youth, I can no longer lead a "normal" love life. I would strongly suggest not getting into the adult business solely for the money. If you care a lot about looking for a long-term relationship, I would also pause and consider your options. Can you make a killing in porn? Yes, absolutely. But there are no guarantees. Can you find the love of your life who also accepts your unique job or past? Sure, absolutely, you could be the exception to the rule. But do not come into porn without at least thinking seriously about these topics. Unlike many other jobs, it's all filmed and online forever. Every employer, family member, and potential mate will be able to watch you have sex, and there are repercussions. I don't mean to come off like I regret my choice, because I don't. I don't believe in regrets. But I do encourage you to think long and hard about making the decision to do adult work; it's a permanent one.

There are so many aspects of my job as a performer that I love and do not take for granted. Alternatively, there are a myriad of complaints and awful consequences that make me second-guess my choice to do porn in the first place. This is my contradictory list: I love that I create artistic content for people from all walks of life to enjoy. This gives me purpose and fulfillment in ways I cannot compare. I hate that the internet, tube sites, parents, and society have made it so easy for uneducated minors to watch content not meant for their eyes.

I adore the luxury of working from home or on fun locations. The freedom it gives me can feel never-ending, and I love that I don't have to leave my cottage. But often, the idea of that freedom outweighs the reality. Having self-motivation without a nine-to-five job or without an on-set call time like the old days can be difficult to muster. Sometimes the pressure of having to make my own schedule leads me into a downward spiral of depression, a battle that I have fought for many years.

I am obsessed with my fans and the #Reigndeer collective that has formed over the years. Their fan art, their kind messages, and their support can be overwhelming in the best possible way. I feel so loved and adored by millions of people. On the flip side lies a terrifying fear that one of them may try to stalk or hurt me. I have given them the illusion that they are close enough to me to ask me anything and exist in an online relationship with me, yet I still have boundaries and restrictions that they may not understand.

The financial opportunities feel endless and full. I can make money from my bed, and at least some of the time, I enjoy taking photos and interacting. But I often contemplate the life span of my "worth" in the adult marketplace. Will it be valuable in five years? In ten years? Is my aging taking away from my value for my fans? I wonder.

While performing in porn, I have enjoyed many days on set of hard labor, physical fulfillment, artistic choices, and the ability to feel free. Freedom is such an important part of my life. Now that I am transitioning into motherhood and life off set, how will my choices affect my daily life? My child's life? My partner's life? Will people's perception of me be forever frozen in the time capsule of the XXX videos I starred in? Will anyone be able to see past this brief moment in my long life ahead? I am repeatedly processing trauma by writing about it and speaking about it, and that can be so painful. I have to be aware of the effect that it has on my depression. "I TOLD YOU SO!" is what stops women from speaking out, so remember not to say it.

I am so grateful for the advocacy work that I have been able to participate in and the real changes I've made to the adult business by speaking up about the injustices within it. Normalizing speaking out about sexual harassment and not being afraid to tell the truth about what is going on behind the scenes will take many other performers, but at least it has started. Being able to use my star power for good has been one of the most rewarding parts of my career.